THE EVERYTHING KIDS' Crazy Puzzles Book

Wild and Wacky Puzzles to Mix Up the Fun!

Beth L. Blair and Jennifer A. Ericsson

Adams Media
Avon, Massachusetts

EDITORIAL
Publishing Director: Gary M. Krebs
Managing Editor: Kate McBride
Copy Chief: Laura M. Daly
Acquisitions Editor: Kate Burgo
Production Editors: Bridget Brace, Jamie Wielgus

PRODUCTION
Production Director: Susan Beale
Production Manager: Michelle Roy Kelly
Series Designers: Colleen Cunningham, Erin Ring
Layout and Graphics: Colleen Cunningham,
    Rachael Eiben, John Paulhus, Daria Perreault,
    Erin Ring
Cover Layout: Paul Beatrice, Matt LeBlanc

An Everything® Series Book.
Everything® and everything.com® are registered trademarks of F+W Publications, Inc.

Published by Adams Media, an F+W Publications Company
57 Littlefield Street, Avon, MA 02322. U.S.A.

ISBN 13: 978-1-59337-361-0
ISBN 10: 1-59337-361-9

Printed in the United States of America.

J I H G F E D C

This publication is designed to provide accurate and authoritative information with regard to the subject matter covered. It is sold with the understanding that the publisher is not engaged in rendering legal, accounting, or other professional advice. If legal advice or other expert assistance is required, the services of a competent professional person should be sought.

—From a *Declaration of Principles* jointly adopted by a Committee of the American Bar Association and a Committee of Publishers and Associations

Many of the designations used by manufacturers and sellers to distinguish their products are claimed as trademarks. When those designations appear in this book and Adams Media was aware of a trademark claim, the designations have been printed with initial capital letters.

Cover illustrations by Dana Regan.
Interior illustrations by Kurt Dolber.
Puzzles by Beth L. Blair.

This book is available at quantity discounts for bulk purchases.
For information, please call 1-800-289-0963.

See the entire Everything® series at *www.everything.com*.

Contents

DEDICATION

To my wild and crazy nephews, Anthony and Austin. —JAE

To Christopher: I'm C-R-A-Z-Y about you! —BLB

Introduction

Are you a kid between the ages of seven and twelve? Do you like to laugh? Do you like to act wacky and silly? If so, then *The Everything® Kids' Crazy Puzzles Book* will be just perfect for you! You'll find word searches and hidden pictures, mazes and math puzzles, scrambles and crisscrosses, and much, much more. All these puzzles look at things that you're familiar with—friendship, hobbies, family, nature, food, travel, parties, and sports—but look at them in a fun and funny way.

Here's an example:

Lots of people run and bike and hike to give their body exercise. But how often do you exercise your face? Why not give it a workout by having a funny face contest with your friends?

Look closely at the picture on the next page. Find the hidden letters on each kid. Put them in order on the lines provided to create the two-word answer to this crazy riddle.

What is yours, but other people use it more than you do?

If you thought that puzzle was fun, flip open the book and try a few more. There are enough peculiar puzzles and ridiculous riddles here to keep you busy and laughing for hours and hours.

Happy puzzling!

Jennifer A. Ericsson
Beth L. Blair

P.S. Be sure to look for Mervin (the mouse). Once again, he's hiding on every single puzzle page (except for vi!). Sometimes he's really big, and sometimes he's really small, but he's always really good at hiding. Look carefully!

_ _ _ _ _ _ _ _ _ !

Chapter 1

Humorous Houses

Houses in Houses

Have you ever thought about all the things in your house that can be found inside something else? See if you can figure out the names of all of the "housemates" listed below. Then fit the names into their proper place in the crisscross grid. We left you a few H-O-U-S-E-S to help!

I live in a frame. _____

I live in a piggybank. _____

I live in a vase. _____

I live in a carton. _____

I live in a tube. _____

I live in a deck. _____

I live in a trashcan. _____

I live in a book. _____

I live in a tank. _____

I live in a jar. _____

I live in a lamp. _____

I live in a box. _____

I live in a hamper. _____

I live in a clock. _____

Knock, Knock!

Who's there? To find out, collect all the words with the same number from the grid and write them in their numbered door. Rearrange the words to get the answer to each door's joke.

1
Knock, knock.
Who's there?
Anita.
Anita who?

?

5 own	2 play?	4 with	2 come	4 you.
3 it's	4 tell	1 minute	3 out	3 up,
1 to	5 name?	4 Ketchup	2 out	5 your
4 I'll	5 know	3 here!	3 Harry	1 over.
2 and	3 cold	1 Anita	4 and	5 Don't
1 think	2 Canoe	5 you	1 it	4 me

2
Knock, knock.
Who's there?
Canoe.
Canoe who?

3
Knock, knock.
Who's there?
Harry.
Harry who?

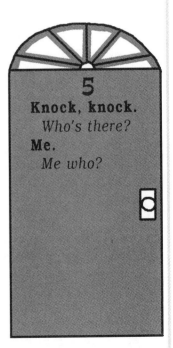

4
Knock, knock.
Who's there?
Ketchup.
Ketchup who?

5
Knock, knock.
Who's there?
Me.
Me who?

No Way!

Pamela has gotten stuck crawling through the fence around her backyard. Her brother says he can't help to get her out. Why? Break the wingding code to find out the reason!

A=✿ B=❂ C=✳ D=☞ E=✒

H=❋ I=✲ N=★ O=❖ R=✚

S=✂ T=✏ U=✪ W=🐭

BECAUSE HE CAN'T BE A BROTHER AND ASSISTER, TOO.

It's impossible!

Silly Sand

Can you find the 11 differences between these two sand castles?

HINT: It doesn't count that they are mirror images.

Muddy Madness

Mom is not happy—there is mud all over her clean kitchen floor! Look carefully at the list of suspects. Can you figure out who made the four sets of tracks?

Next time, WIPE YOUR FEET!

SUSPECTS

hamster

turtle

cat

snake

kangaroo

chicken

goose

dog

elephant

mouse

Name Game

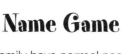

The people in this family have normal names, but they sure have a strange way of acting out what they are! Match each name in the list to the correct family member.

Alexis José Angelina Matt Noah
Art Carol Abigail Mark Isaac

HARK THE HERALD ANGELS SING...

Dog in the House

These words are all missing a few letters. Figure out which letters to add so that you end up with the names of eight different places in which you might live!

EXTRA FUN: Collect the letters you added. Use them to spell the name of a familiar small and curly dog. Write this pet's name on the lines below.

_ _ _ _ _ _ _ _

_ _ _ _ _

H _ U S _

B _ A T

_ R A _ L E R

A _ A _ T _ E _ T

H O T _ _

C _ B _ N

_ _ P L E X

Shy Pets

Can you find the 12 animals hidden in these sentences? Look carefully—some of these animals are not normally found in a house!

HINT: We circled the first pet for you.

Can't you catch me?
We allow lots of oxygen here.
The sad ogre ate chili on toast.
I wish arks were floating in my pond.
"Woof" is how Max says hello.
Please grab bits of drab earth.
Caspar rotated the extra tires on his car.

7

That's Different!

Put the missing words from each rhyme into the proper spaces. Then connect the dots to see what kind of unusual houses you have built!

I come _____ so I can _____.
I'm covered with _____ that
won't unravel. I'm built on
_____ stuck in the _____ —
the sticks are _____, but
my _____ is round!

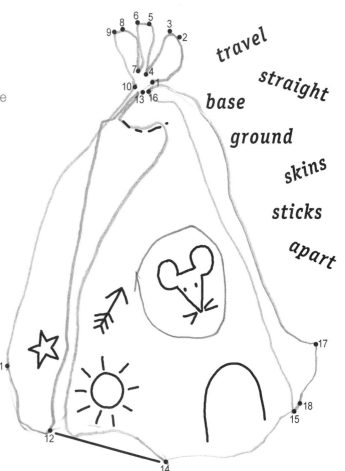

travel
straight
base
ground
skins
sticks
apart

I'm icy _____ and made of
snow. Outside my _____
it's 10 _____! I'm built
from _____, but my
_____ is round.
Where it's _____,
I won't be _____!

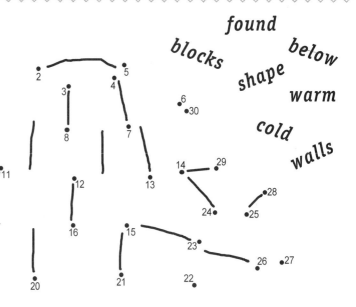

found
blocks
shape
below
warm
cold
walls

Tidy Cat

Answer as many clues as you can and fill the letters into the grid. Work back and forth between the box and the clues to find the answer to the crazy question.

A. The ninth letter

$\dfrac{I}{7}$

B. Holds up pants

$\overline{12}$ $\overline{5}$ $\overline{6}$ $\overline{3}$

C. The way out

$\overline{10}$ $\overline{14}$ $\overline{1}$ $\overline{9}$

D. Opposite of south

$\overline{2}$ $\overline{13}$ $\overline{11}$ $\overline{8}$ $\overline{4}$

Where does a crazy house cat hide the family's garbage?

1C	2D		3B	4D	5B	
6B	7A	8D	9C	10C	11D	
12B	13D	14C	!			

EXTRA FUN: Look for the following 10 items hiding in the trash: banana, glove, capital letter H, fried egg, hanger, cat, fish, umbrella, fish hook, and Mervin, of course!

Who Lives Where?

Unscramble the list of five rather unusual places to live. Then put the number of each house next to the crazy character who lives there!

EXTRA FUN: Fill in all the squares with a dot in the upper right-hand corner to see where the last crazy character lives.

1. HILGT HOUSE

2. RBID HOUSE

3. ARCD HOUSE

4. ETAHUND HOUSE

5. ERGBREGADIN HOUSE

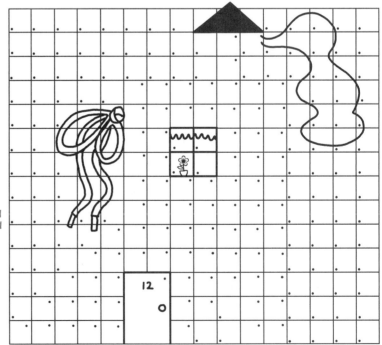

What's Weird?

Can you find the 16 things that are not quite normal in this house?

The Ha-Ha House

Match a number with a letter to get a joke and its answer!

END

A The outside!

3 How can paint make a cold house warmer?

2 "Our next door neighbor is on the phone."

B It was having windowpanes!

1 _
2 _
3 _
4 _
5 _
6 _

1 Does a snake's house have a big cellar?

4 If people live in condos, where do ducks live?

C Put on two coats!

5 What side of a house gets the most rain?

D Pondos!

6 Why did the old house go to the doctor?

E "That's a close call!"

F No, just a crawl space!

Find Mervin's path from START to END.

START

12

Chapter 2

Fritzy Friends

Autograph Fun

Some clever friends have signed this page with rebus autographs.
Can you figure out these silly sentiments?

_ GOOD
_ B
_ SOON
_ GOTTEN

U R A 10 !

A+ U

M+ +

Yours till the...

+S

or the

+S

or the

+S!

Loony Language

Aidan and Nadia are best friends with their own special language. Can you figure out what they are saying? **HINT:** Think opposites!

Goodbye, Nadia.
What are me down to?

Goodbye, Aidan. You just got in of school.

Did I have a bad night?

Yes! You had too few tests.

That's too good.
Yesterday will be
the same.

You hope not!

Well, you have
to stay. Hello!

Hello!

Goodbye! How are I?

You am bad!

Friendly Hink Pinks

The answers to Hink Pinks are rhyming words with the same number of syllables. Think of words that mean the same as "friend," and see if you can figure these out.

A girl friend

_ _ _

_ _ _

A dirty friend

_ _ _ _ _

_ _ _ _ _

A wonderful friend

_ _ _ _ _

_ _ _ _ _

A sad friend

_ _ _ _

_ _ _ _

Almost Twins

Mary and Myra are such good friends that they wish they were twins. Many days they try to dress exactly alike. Today, they do look very similar, but there are 10 things that are different about their outfits. Can you find them all?

Looks the Same, But . . .

Can you think of two different ways to pronounce each of these words?

bass   **lead**   **wind**

bow   **sewer**   **tear**

Bead Buddies

Ivy and Lilly made friendship bracelets out of lettered beads. Only they know what the letters spell out when they are read in the correct order! Start at the bead with the dot. Move clockwise around the bracelet picking up every third letter. Write the letters on the lines to learn what these two friends always say to each other.

_ _ _ _

_ _ _ _ _

Just Friends

This is weird—Josh has 21 friends and all their names start with the letter J! Can you find them in this word search? How many are boys? How many are girls?

J	E	R	E	M	I	A	H	O	O	J	J	U	Y
O	I	R	E	F	I	N	N	E	J	U	O	W	D
H	O	O	J	O	L	O	J	U	O	W	A	L	U
N	U	J	I	J	I	J	I	J	S	O	N	I	J

					U	J	U	L	I	E			
					J	I	L	I	N	W			
					A	N	J	J	O	E			
					N	J	O	A	O	L			
					N	I	T	S	U	J			
					A	G	I	O	A	E			
					U	I	J	N	N	S			

S	J	O			O	J	U	O	U	S
E	O	D	J		J	I	I	U	J	E
M	W	E	I	X	I	L	J	G	L	N	O
A	I	J	A	C	K	U	O	A	E	J	L	O
J	J	G	W	L	O	Y	O	C	L	A	N	J
	G	E	D	A	J	I	J	O	S	I	E
		E	I	U	U	G	O	B	G	N	O
		J	A	N	E	T	I	O	J

Get your lemonade here!

1 SIZE – 35¢ LEMONADE

Pucker Up!

ICE COLD LEMONADE!

Josie and Arlo have lemonade stands across the street from each other. If they both sell all of their cups of lemonade, who will make the most money?

Lemonade large 50¢ small 25¢

Crazy Keyboard

Kayla is e-mailing a funny joke to all of her friends, but her keyboard is acting weird. The letters she types are not the letters that appear on the screen! Can you crack the code to see what joke will make Kayla's friends LOL (Laugh Out Loud)?

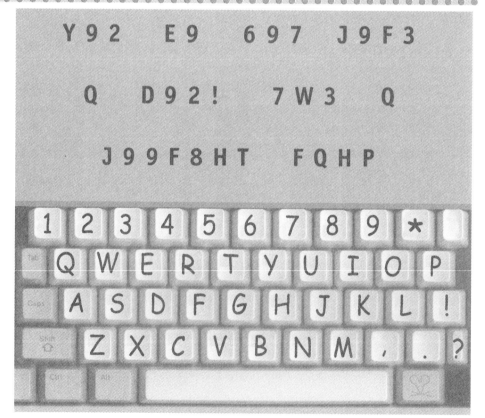

Y 9 2   E 9   6 9 7   J 9 F 3

Q   D 9 2 !   7 W 3   Q

J 9 9 F 8 H T   F Q H P

Tough for Two

There are many games that are impossible to play with only one other friend. The names of these games have been broken in two. After you have matched up the two halves, fit the name into its proper place in the crisscross. We've left you some G-A-M-E-S to get you started.

JUMP

RELAY

BALL

PYRA

LIM

MONKEY IN

PHONE

FOUR

TELE

MID

ROPE

SAYS

DODGE

SIMON

BO

THE MIDDLE

RACE

SQUARE

Silly Sleepover

Missy and Chrissy have chosen a very odd place to have their sleepover! Follow the directions to find out where they are.

Find box 1-A and copy it into square 1-A in the grid.

Find box 1-B and copy it into square 1-B in the grid.

Continue doing this until you have copied all the boxes into the grid.

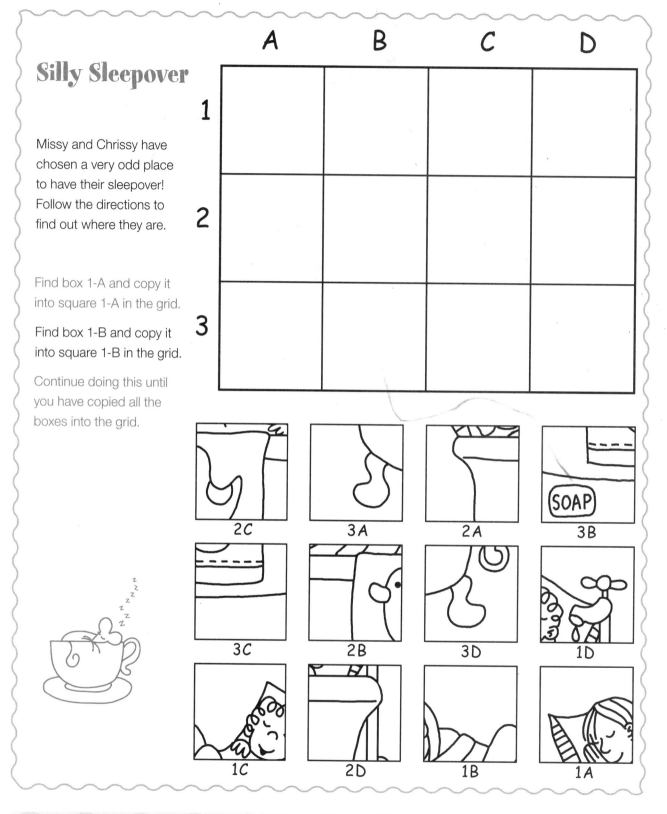

20

Pass It On

Parker tried to pass this funny joke to Toshi during math class. When he got caught, Parker ripped up the note. Can you piece it back together so you can have a good laugh, too? Write the fixed-up joke on the blank piece of paper.

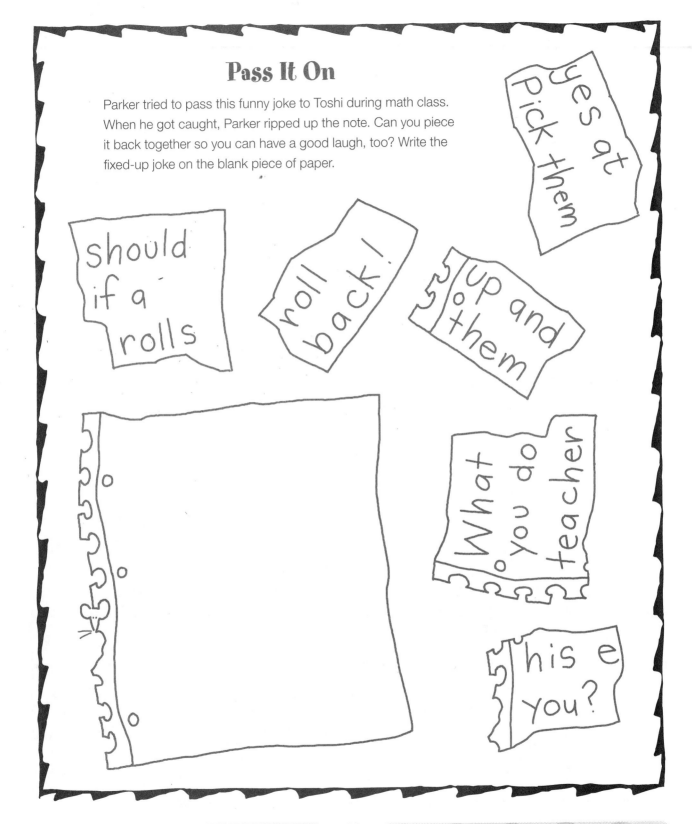

yes at pick them

should if a rolls

roll back!

up and them

What you do teacher

his e you?

Ready, Set, Go!

Griffin and Aubrey are racing to the library. Griffin can hop only on odd-numbered squares that touch each other. Aubrey can glide only on even-numbered squares that touch! The race starts at Griffin's house. Who will use the fewest squares to get to the library?

HINT: Enter buildings at the white triangles.

Tasty Pastry		Bud's Florist		Home Run Sports	38	8	16	12	40	10	22	Harry's Pottery

Tasty Pastry · Bud's Florist · Home Run Sports

38 | 8 | 16 | 12 | 40 | 10 | 22 | Harry's Pottery

4 | Hair Flair | 13 | Post Office | 18

84 | 7 | 114 | 26 | 32 | 12 | 13 | 51 | 22 | 20 | 8 | 6 | 44

75 | Library | 17 | Movieland | 20 | Pete's Pets | 14 | Park

93 | Library | 62 | NOW SHOWING | 12 | 41 | 6 | 100 | 12

9 | 43 | 31 | 40 | 23 | 21 | 13 | 11 | 37 | 42 | Deep Blue Computer Store | 4

8 | Doh Nuts | 53 | All-Nite Diner | 19 | Lots o' Pizza | 33 | Renta Movie | 11 | 48

21 | Doh Nuts | 17 | All-Nite Diner | 7 | Lots o' Pizza | 17 | Renta Movie | 12 | 2

42 | 11 | 19 | All-Nite Diner | 15 | 22 | 339 | 71 | 9 | 37 | 3 | START

83 | 47 | 217 | 3 | Fire Station #9 | Shop n' Shop Grocery | 4 | Griffin's House

Parkside Elem. School | 13

26

In the Shadows

Mieko and Harry are making shadow puppets on the wall. Can you find the pattern that exactly matches the picture to the right?

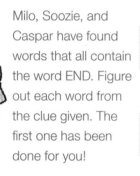

Friends to the End

Milo, Soozie, and Caspar have found words that all contain the word END. Figure out each word from the clue given. The first one has been done for you!

F R I E N D = a person you like who likes you

_ E N D = to let a person borrow something

_ _ E N D = to mix together completely

_ _ E N D = to pay money

S P _ E N D _ _ = pale purple

_ E N D = to fix or repair

_ E N D _ _ = kind or loving

_ _ E N D _ = a list of things to be done

_ _ _ E N D = to protect against danger

_ _ _ E N D = to make longer

_ _ _ E N D = story told for many years

_ _ _ E N D = to cause to be angry

E N D _ _ _ _ = never stopping

_ _ E N D _ _ = long and thin

_ _ _ E N D _ _ = info at the end of a book

_ _ _ E N D _ _ = place to write special dates

_ _ _ E N D _ _ = really awesome

_ E N D _ _ = metal piece over a bike's wheel

Chapter 3

Peculiar Parties

Birthday Bowling

Nayib is celebrating his birthday at the bowling alley. How old do you think he is?

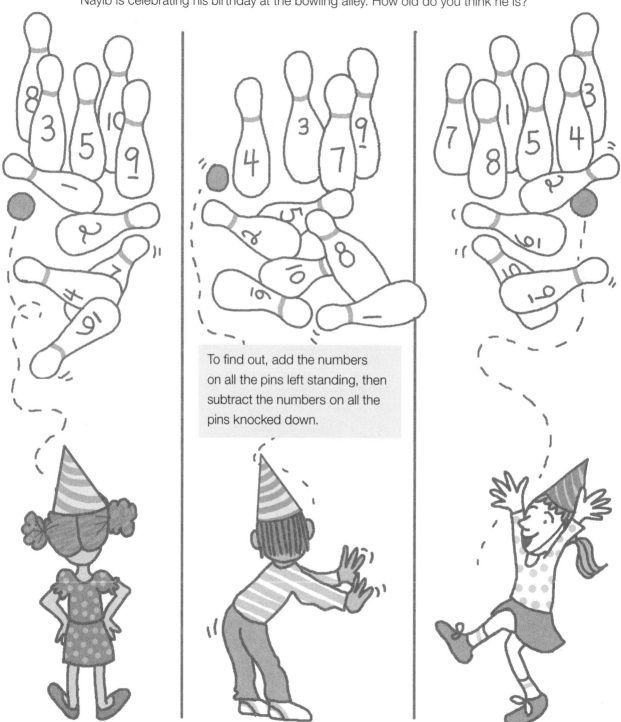

To find out, add the numbers on all the pins left standing, then subtract the numbers on all the pins knocked down.

Happy Half

Something is wrong with Hunter's instant camera. Only one half of each picture comes out! Can you help him by drawing in the rest of each party picture?

Peculiari-tea

Tanika invited four friends to a tea party, but each guest wanted something different to drink! Break the code on each cup to see what kind of drinks Tanika made for her guests.

Hink Pinks

The answers to these riddles are two single-syllable words that rhyme. Can you figure out these party hink pinks?

A quick present = _ _ _ _ _   _ _ _ _

A not real dessert = _ _ _ _   _ _ _ _

A dumb party activity = _ _ _ _   _ _ _ _

Kooky Carnival

How many weird or wacky things can you find at this backyard carnival?

Cake-o-licious

Everyone has their favorite kind of cake. What sort of cake do you think each of these characters likes best? When you have decided, see if you can fit the cake names into the puzzle grid. We left you a B-I-T-E of I-C-I-N-G to get you started!

Why Do Candles . . .

Drop the letters into their proper place in the grid. The letters in each column fit in the spaces directly underneath that column, but they may be scrambled. Once you have them in their correct spots, you will know the answer to this silly riddle:

Why do candles go on top of a birthday cake?

What Should You . . .

The four words that make up the answer to this riddle are hiding in this picture. Once you find them, put them in the correct order and write the answer in the colored box.

What should you do if your birthday cake tastes burnt and crunchy?

You're Invited!

Hannah is having a party and sent this eccentric invitation to all of her friends. Can you read the invitation, and figure out what kind of party Hannah is having?

EXTRA FUN: Guess why Hannah chose this kind of party!

> Please come to my party!
> Date: Saturday, April 1
> Time: 5–7 p.m.
> Place: 3223 Eva Ave.
> Acaloola, CA
> Breakfast will be served.
> Wear your clothes backward!
> Hannah Anna

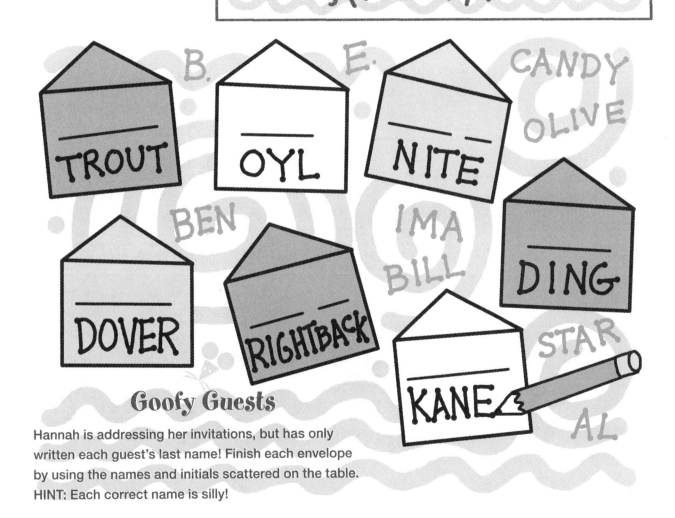

B. E. CANDY OLIVE BEN IMA BILL STAR AL

TROUT OYL NITE DING DOVER RIGHTBACK KANE

Goofy Guests

Hannah is addressing her invitations, but has only written each guest's last name! Finish each envelope by using the names and initials scattered on the table.
HINT: Each correct name is silly!

Crazy Costume

Chloe is having a hard time deciding what to wear to Zoe's costume party. Use the clues to figure out what Chloe finally decided to wear. Circle her choices.

HINT: The party has an "ocean" theme!

She did not wear boots or clogs.

She did wear a dress, but it did not have polka dots.

She did wear something on her head, but it wasn't a hat.

She did wear something around her neck, but it wasn't a scarf.

She did carry something, but it wasn't an umbrella.

Silly Song

It is traditional to sing to a person on his or her birthday. Use the note decoder to figure out some loony lyrics that you might like to try at your next birthday party!

Balls of String

There's an extra letter hiding several times in each row. Take it out, and you will leave behind the name of a classic party game! Write each hidden letter on the blank line for that row. Read down the letters to answer this riddle:

Two balls of string ran a race. Which one won?

___ mtutsicatl cthatirts
___ bhlhihnd mhahn's hbhlufhf
___ esiemoen esaeyes
___ byinygyo
___ cwhawrawdes
___ feolleow thee eleeaeder
___ rrerd lrigrht rgreren rlrigrht
___ eleeaepferog
___ thot ptotattot
___ iduick diuicki goiosie
___ heidee eande eseeke
___ dstatdudes

Find Your Way

from balloon to cake!

Start

End

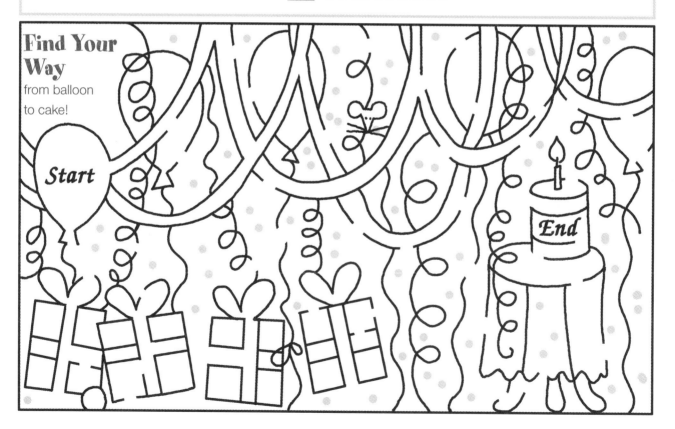

Looking for Loot

This band of party pirates is looking for treasure. Start at number 1 and connect the dots in order to see where they finally found their goodie bags.

EXTRA FUN: After you have connected the dots, use a green crayon or marker to add some important details to finish the picture!

35

Tons of Fun

You can plan a party around any theme or for any occasion! Can you find all 50 party ideas hidden in this word search?

```
S R U A S O N I D H I P P I E L G N U J
W M M A C A R N I V A L X P A J A M A S
I Y A B H C E O X A E S E H T R E D N U
M S E C R E T A G E N T S P I Z Z A O S
M T R P I B S S D B E G N I T A K S T T
I E C R S A R T S A N D C R A F T S R H
N R E I T R E R E L I H W A S O E I A G
G Y C N M B T O I L T I S T W S D L V I
G N I C A E N P V E N P E E H Y L L E N
N E D E S C I S O R E P X S X O O Y L K
I E W S D U W S M I L Y A D H T R I B D
V W C S B E A C H N A C I G A M A S E N
I O O R O L A F A A V D A N C I N G E A
G L O E S R D W W S H A N U K K A H C S
S L K T S O E C A P S R E T U O S I A N
K A I S O C O M I C B O O K S L R X M O
N H E A D X W W I L D W E S T C L D P G
A T S E I F E D A L S X L B U G S W I A
H S L L O D M O N S T E R S U O S X N R
T S E O R E H R E P U S F I S H I N G D
```

arts and crafts

barbecue

beach

fiesta

Hawaiian

jungle

monsters

mystery

pirates

pizza

swimming

secret agents

Thanksgiving

outer space

birthday

circus

camping

dragons and knights

Christmas

cookies

Wild West	Hanukkah	horses	dancing	princess	travel
ballerinas	under the sea	comic books	skating	fishing	silly
dinosaurs	Valentine	movies	Halloween	toys	ice cream
Easter	carnival	cars	winter	hippie	magic
superheroes	sports	pets	pajamas	bugs	dolls

Chapter 4

Funny Food

Soup's On!

It seems some very strange items have fallen into each of these pots of soup. Can you cross out the ingredients you would NEVER find in soup? Then look at the remaining ingredients and see if you can tell what kind of soup is in each pot.

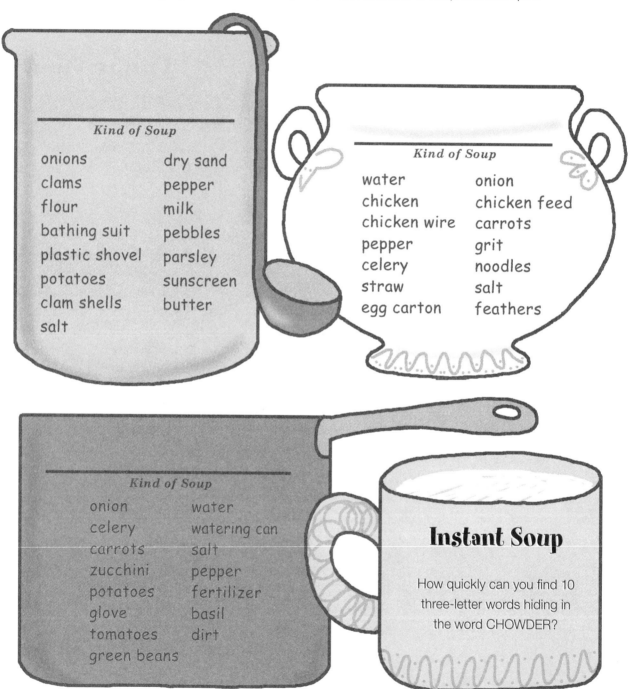

Kind of Soup

onions	dry sand
clams	pepper
flour	milk
bathing suit	pebbles
plastic shovel	parsley
potatoes	sunscreen
clam shells	butter
salt	

Kind of Soup

water	onion
chicken	chicken feed
chicken wire	carrots
pepper	grit
celery	noodles
straw	salt
egg carton	feathers

Kind of Soup

onion	water
celery	watering can
carrots	salt
zucchini	pepper
potatoes	fertilizer
glove	basil
tomatoes	dirt
green beans	

Instant Soup

How quickly can you find 10 three-letter words hiding in the word CHOWDER?

38

What a Mouthful

Is this a secret code? No, each food is simply listed by its dictionary pronunciation! Write the more familiar spelling of each name in the empty spaces.

ap´ əl sôs

_____

kū´ kum bər

_____

sī´ dər

_____

bə nan´ ə

_____

kô´ lə flou´ ər

_____

brok´ ə lē

_____

cher´ ē

_____

säl´ sə

_____

sə lä´ mē

_____

av´ ə kä´ dō

_____

bā´ ken

_____

Berry Good

Each berry in this garden uses two sets of letters. Can you match the letter sets to find all the berries? Be careful—there's one extra letter set!

_ _ _ _ _ _ BERRY

_ _ _ _ BERRY

_ _ _ _ _ _ BERRY

_ _ _ _ _ BERRY

_ _ _ _ _ BERRY

_ _ _ _ _ BERRY

BL CR CK RA

STR GO BLA HU SP OSE UE AN AW

Put a different letter from the list into each empty box to make a familiar cooking word. The empty box might be at the beginning, the middle, or the end of the mystery word. **HINT:** Each letter in the list will be used only once.

When you are done, read down the shaded boxes to discover the answer to this curious cooking question:

Where should you go if you are a really, really bad cook?

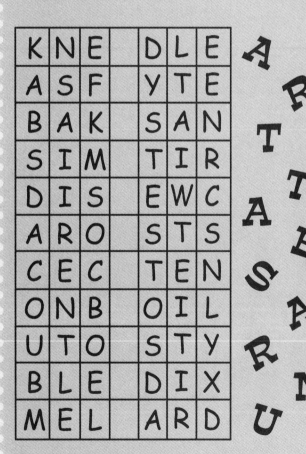

K	N	E		D	L	E
A	S	F		Y	T	E
B	A	K		S	A	N
S	I	M		T	I	R
D	I	S		E	W	C
A	R	O		S	T	S
C	E	C		T	E	N
O	N	B		O	I	L
U	T	O		S	T	Y
B	L	E		D	I	X
M	E	L		A	R	D

A R T T E A S A R U N

Dizzy Donuts

The Kruller family bought a baker's dozen donuts. Can you tell, by using the following clues, how many donuts each person ate? **HINT:** A baker's dozen = 13.

- Dad ate twice as many donuts as Mom.
- Brooke ate fewer donuts than everyone else.
- Austin and Caleb ate the same number of donuts

EXTRA FUN: Someone has taken a bite—and a letter—out of each of these donuts! Can you figure out what kinds of donuts were tasted?

Splash!

The ship's cook dropped dinner in the drink! Can you help him find his soggy supper? Look for a piece of cheese on a cracker, orange slice, apple, bowl of spaghetti, bowl of salad, slice of bread, stick of butter, glass of water, ice-cream cone, salt shaker, knife, fork, spoon, and teacup.

Crazy Cookies

Can you find the two cookies that are decorated with the exact same face?

What meal do you eat if it's too late for breakfast, but too early for lunch?

Use the descriptions below to help you figure out the names of six familiar foods that are good for breakfast or lunch. Read the letters in the shaded boxes to spell the answer to this riddle:

Serve this round bread with cream cheese = ▨ _ _ _ _

Pour milk over this crunchy food = _ _ ▨ _ _ _ _

This dairy product comes in little cups = _ _ _ ▨ _ _

This familiar food is also called a "flapjack" = _ _ ▨ _ _ _ _

You must squeeze an orange to get this = _ _ _ ▨ _

A slice of this smoked meat is good with eggs = ▨ _ _

What's the Difference . . .

Answer as many clues below as you can and fill the numbered letters into the grid.
Work back and forth between the grid and the clues until you find the answer to
the riddle. **HINT:** The black boxes are the spaces between words.

What's the difference between an elephant and a chocolate-chip cookie?

1G	2F	3B		4D	5H	6B		7F

8B	9C	10G	11D			12H	13H

14A **E**	15E	16B	17E	18F	19A **A**	20A **N**	21G

22D	23H		24C	25C	26E	27B

28A **M**	29G	30E	31D	!

A. Not nice

$\underline{\text{M}}$ $\underline{\text{E}}$ $\underline{\text{A}}$ $\underline{\text{N}}$
28 14 19 20

B. Opposite of over

___ ___ ___ ___ ___
3 6 8 16 27

C. Opposite of me

___ ___ ___
24 25 9

D. Hit with your foot

___ ___ ___ ___
31 22 4 11

E. Opposite of push

___ ___ ___ ___
17 26 30 15

F. Opposite of cold

___ ___ ___
18 2 7

G. Really small

___ ___ ___ ___
21 29 10 1

H. Another name
for Grandma

___ ___ ___ ___
13 5 23 12

Second Helpings

Each food name in this puzzle has a double letter in it. Some names have two sets of double letters! Write the answer to each clue in the crossword grid on the next page. We left the double letters to give you a hand.

ACROSS

3 Smooth and creamy dessert served in a bowl

5 Hot tomato and cheese pie served in triangles

7 Breakfast food covered with little squares

8 Sometimes this is inside a roast chicken

11 Creamy drink made in a blender from milk, fruit, and ice

12 This gets sliced on pizza, or tossed in salads

15 Fluffy, sweet and golden bread made with many eggs

17 Italian pasta you twirl on a fork

19 Prickly golden fruit with stiff green leaves on top

24 Small, round fruits that grow on bushes

25 Leafy vegetable used to make salads

26 A sweet treat eaten after a meal

27 Dark colored soda that's not cola

28 Fragrant spice often used in Christmas cookies

DOWN

1 Tasty dip made from chickpeas

2 Long, flat pasta made from flour and egg

4 Hard, golden candy made from butter, sugar, and cream

6 These long, green vegetables grow like crazy in the summer

9 Sweet treats made on a stick

10 Mexican flat bread used to wrap around food

12 Small breakfast cakes

13 Cooked spheres of hamburger, egg, and spices

14 Round, flat, baked treats

16 Mervin loves this dairy product that's sometimes sliced and sometimes stretchy.

18 Crunchy Chinese "tube" filled with vegetables and meat

20 Vegetable that looks like a tree

21 Dairy product you can melt or spread

22 Round, red vegetables that grow underground

23 Small, round, red fruits with long stems

S·L·L·L·L·U·U·U·R·R·R·P!

Follow Rosie's super-long strand of pasta over and under from her slurping lips to the meatball at the bottom of the plate!

START

END

How Do You Make . . .

The new kid working at the snack bar is still learning his job. Look closely at the menu. Can you find the answer to his question?

How do you make a hotdog roll?

hoT dog   **YOgurt**   **chiPs**

Ice cream   **hambURger**   **grilLed cheese**

miLk   **sAlad**

Tuna fish   **Taco**

                    french friEs

Fill 'er Up!

The average person in America eats about 29 bowls of this tasty treat every year! Fill in all the shapes that have the letter C, R, U, N, C, or H to find the name of this popular snack.

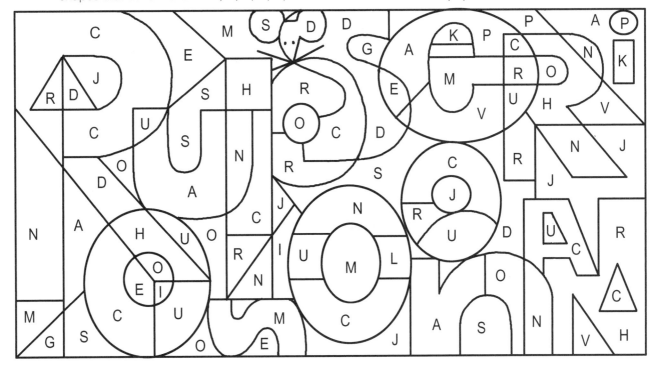

Scrambled Eggs

Each of these character's favorite meal has been broken into three pieces and scrambled around the page. Can you match up the parts and make silly-sounding breakfasts for everyone? Write your answers on the empty lines.

OF

LEGS

AND

WHEAT

BACON

SCREAM

LES

OF

WO

Leftovers

Write a word from the shaded column next to a word in the left column to make the name of a familiar food. There may be more than one way to match up all the words—just make sure there are no leftovers!

I've got my part!

I have my part, too!

CUP _____
STRAW _____
POTATO _____
PEANUT _____
POP _____
CORN _____
COLE _____
HOT _____
HAM _____
FRENCH _____
TUNA _____
APPLE _____
EGG _____

FRIES
MELT
SAUCE
ROLL
BURGER
BERRY
CORN
BUTTER
CAKE
SALAD
SLAW
CHIPS
DOG

Chapter 5

Hysterical Hobbies

Daffy Descriptions

Even the most normal hobby can sound strange when you try to describe it! Can you identify all the hobbies below? We left you a few H-I-N-T-S to help out.

7. Taking a variety of unprepared foods and making them ready to eat

8. Keeping balls in continuous motion from your hands to the air by skillful tossing and catching

9. Using the keys on a wooden instrument to produce various melodic sounds

10. Gathering together a variety of human-like toys

11. Controlling a paper shape in the sky at the end of a long string

12. Moving through the water by using your arms and legs

1. Riding a low, flat board with wheels on the bottom

2. Using a rod, reel, and hook to catch aquatic creatures

3. Rolling a large ball and knocking down wooden pins

4. Practicing the Japanese art of folding paper to make small sculptures

5. Fitting together small pieces of a picture to recreate the entire big picture

6. Using your legs to power a vehicle with two wheels

EXTRA FUN: What would you call a giant ape whose hobby is table tennis? Read down the shaded column to find out!

Take a Hike

A riddle and its answer were put into the large grid, and then cut into seven pieces. See if you can figure out where each piece goes, and write the letters in their proper places. When you have filled the grid in correctly, you will be able to read the puzzle from left to right, and top to bottom. **HINT:** The black boxes stand for the spaces between words.

Tacky Ties

Dad has some pretty tacky ties in his collection. Today he is hunting for one in particular. Can you help him find it? Look for the tie that has all of the following:

- dark diamonds
- light background
- skinny horizontal stripes
- same-sized polka dots

Too Much Fun

This person has a LOT of hobbies! Can you tell how many he is trying to do at the same time?

Cool Collections

Can you find nine things in this word search that you might want to collect, and nine things that you would probably never collect?

```
S T A M P S H O V E G
F O O S H B I N G P O
F L O C O I N S C A L
X J E L L Y F I S H O
T Y P E S H E L L S H
O K R O W E M O H T A
M A R B L E S M I L E
B A N A T I S S U E S
F O H A T S D U S K Y
S L L O D L P E A S N
O P A L G R E E N Q U
L I G H T B U L B S P
R U N T R R O C K S I
Q S T A P L E S A N D
N O T S E L D O O N O
O V E R D U C A R D S
C O T T O N C A N D Y
S K O O B W O R M S T
```

Might Collect:

Would Never Collect:

Absurd Authors

Levi loves to read—especially about his hobbies!
Write each author's number next to the book they wrote.

Books:
- Learn to Draw
- Hiking Fun
- Veggies A to Z
- Make YOUR OWN Website
- Your Camera
- Butterfly Basics
- MONSTER MADNESS

Authors:
1. Rocky Slopes
2. Dot Comm
3. Annette N. Ajar
4. Brock O. Lee
5. U. Ken Klick
6. Frank N. Stein
7. Art X. Ibit

Camera Chaos

Bryant's new hobby is photography. He tried to take pictures of his visit to the zoo, but he only got part of the animal in each of his shots. What were the animals he was trying to capture on film?

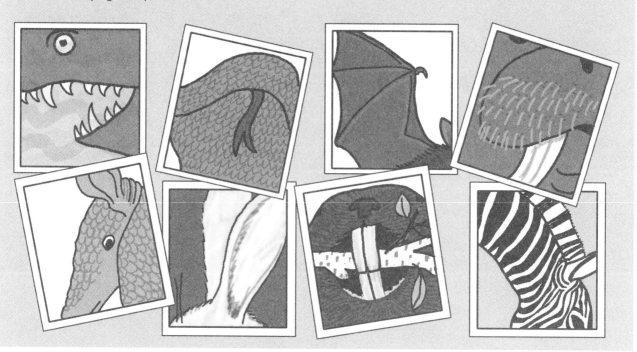

Movie Night

First answer all the clues. After you fill the answers in the numbered grid, collect the letters in the shaded boxes. Unscramble them to find out what movie Kristen and her friends went to see!

ACROSS

4 White, fluffy kernels served with butter and salt

6 The way out

7 Surface on which the movie shows

8 Sweet treats

10 A person you like who likes you back

DOWN

1 Small piece of paper that lets you in

2 You pay with this to get in

3 A sweet and fizzy drink

5 A little laugh

7 Where you sit in the theater

9 What it is when the lights go out

EXTRA FUN: After doing this puzzle, can you guess what Kristen and her friend's three hobbies are?

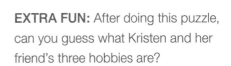

Whittle Away

Wally's hobby is carving tiny sculptures from bars of soap! See if you can find the four different items that Wally plans to create.

EXTRA FUN:
Can you find the letters S, O, A, and P hiding in these bars?

Totally Tiles

Tanika's hobby is creating pictures made from tiny colored tiles glued onto a board. This is called making a mosaic (mo-zay-ik). Color in all the squares marked with the letters T-I-L-E-S and you will see Tanika's latest project!

EXTRA FUN: To finish the picture, connect the dots A, B, and C in order. Then connect the dots 1, 2, and 3 in order.

D	F	G	K	J	F	J	F	M	P	F	G	F	D	K	F
F	T	I	L	N	G	N	G	N	R	G	M	T	I	E	G
G	E	F	T	S	M	R	J	D	U	J	S	L	F	I	J
J	S	M	F	R	T	X	K	O	V	E	P	D	K	L	K
F	T	L	I	X	D	I	M	P	L	K	V	T	E	S	M
K	G	P	O	T	P	S	N	D	S	M	E	K	O	G	N
M	J	D	U	K	I	T	O	V	E	S	J	O	U	D	O
F	K	V	G	O	T	L	I	E	L	L	N	U	G	M	P
N	M	J	M	E	Z	O	P	X	P	N	I	G	D	P	R
O	N	F	S	U	H	I	R	F	L	O	R	T	M	V	U
A	O	N	L	J	F	B	U	G	R	P	X	I	P	F	1
F	P	R	I	N	K	S	L	T	S	R	D	L	V	K	X
K	R	X	T	R	O	B	I	E	2	U	F	E	J	O	V
C	U	F	E	X	U	P	V	J	U	V	K	S	N	U	3
U	V	K	P	T	B	D	X	K	V	D	T	M	R	G	F
V	W	F	V	O	I	E	L	T	S	I	O	P	X	M	G
D	X	O	U	D	N	Q	F	M	X	F	D	V	F	D	J

Milo's Magic

Connect the dots to see what Milo has learned to pull out of his magic hat! To finish the picture, put a dime on each of the dots without numbers, and trace around them.

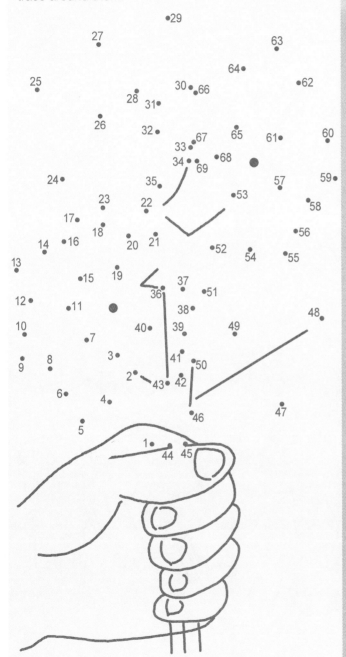

Go Fly a Kite

Kaity's hobby is flying kites. She's not alone—kite flying is popular all over the world! See if you can fit all of the words into this story about Kaity and her kite. **HINT:** Each word gets used only once!

—WORDS—
sight • delight • tight
bright • might • right
height • fright • white • kite

Kaity's kite was red and _____.

To her _____, it flew to a

great _____. She hung on

_____ with all her _____,

but the kite veered sharply to

the _____. Snap went the

string! "Oh, no!" Kaity cried with

_____, as her _____

new _____ flew out of

_____.

Loony Tunes

Curtis invited his musical friends to come play their instruments at his house for the afternoon. But what is wrong with this picture? Can you find the 15 things that are definitely very strange?

Sticky Stamps

Artie dropped his stamp collection and needs help resorting them!
See if you can answer the following questions:

1. Are there more patriotic stamps or stamps with birds?

2. What kind of creature is featured on the most stamps?

3. There are four stamps that are almost identical. What object is on each one?

4. What stamp has the most postage?

Is camping your hobby? Then you know that each camper going on a trip needs to bring some of the gear. But who brings what? Use the multiplying code to find out the answer!

What do you ask an octopus to bring on camping trips?

80 32 56 80 - 8 24 48 32 72

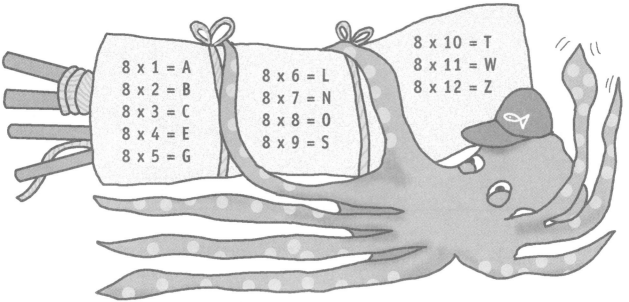

8 x 1 = A
8 x 2 = B
8 x 3 = C
8 x 4 = E
8 x 5 = G

8 x 6 = L
8 x 7 = N
8 x 8 = O
8 x 9 = S

8 x 10 = T
8 x 11 = W
8 x 12 = Z

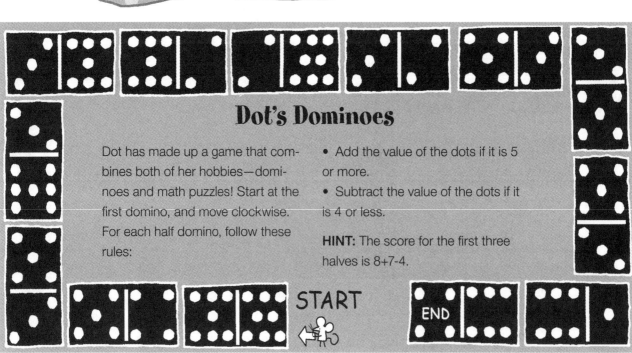

Dot's Dominoes

Dot has made up a game that combines both of her hobbies—dominoes and math puzzles! Start at the first domino, and move clockwise. For each half domino, follow these rules:

• Add the value of the dots if it is 5 or more.

• Subtract the value of the dots if it is 4 or less.

HINT: The score for the first three halves is 8+7-4.

START

END

Chapter 6

Spazzy Sports

Loopy Hoops

These teams have just finished a close game. Who won? Add the numbers on each team's shirts plus the numbers hiding on each team's players, to find out. In this crazy game, it is the team with the least number of points that wins!

DARK SHIRTS:

LIGHT SHIRTS:

Happy Camper

This camper went without sleep for seven days and was never tired. How did he do that? To find out, answer the clues below and enter the letters into the grid.

1D	2B		3A	4C	5D	6A	7C	
	8A	9B		10B	11C	12A	13B	14C

A. Spaces where something is missing __ __ __ __
12 8 6 3

B. Opposite of now __ __ __ __
9 13 2 10

C. To make crooked __ __ __ __
14 11 4 7

D. Opposite of she __ __
1 5

Color in all the following kinds of letters:
- last letter of READY
- first letter of SET
- both letters of GO

Then read the uncolored letters to get the answer to the crazy riddle!

What should you put on before you get dressed to be in a relay race?

```
YOSRGUGYO
NYOSGYSOG
SGDYOOEYG
SSGOYSGOY
OROYSWGYE
OSYAGORYO
```

Why does everyone want spiders on their baseball team?

Pick up letters as you find the correct way through the web and around the bases from HIT to HOME RUN. Write them down in order and you will learn the answer to this riddle!

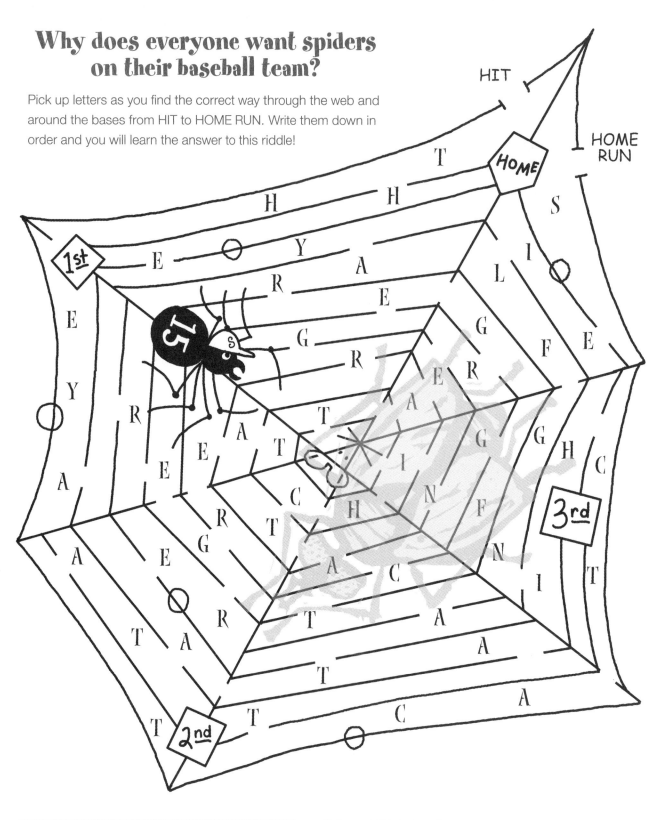

Which ghost cheers the loudest at the high school football games?

To find out, unscramble these common football terms. Write the words in the spaces at the end of each line. Finally, read the letters in the white boxes from top to bottom.

1. Player wears this on his head = METHEL   _ _ _ _ _ _

2. Score! = CHDOTOUWN   _ _ _ _ _ _ _ _ _

3. To handle clumsily = LEBMUF   _ _ _ _ _ _

4. To bring a player to the ground = CAKTEL   _ _ _ _ _ _

5. Shirt with a number on it = SERJYE   _ _ _ _ _ _

6. To receive the ball = CHATC   _ _ _ _ _

7. Midway through the game = METIHAFL   _ _ _ _ _ _ _ _

8. Important January game = PRUES LOWB   _ _ _ _ _ _ _ _ _

9. Throw ball to another player = SAPS   _ _ _ _

10. Catch ball meant for other team = CEPTERINT   _ _ _ _ _ _ _ _ _

11. Three feet = DAYR   _ _ _ _

12. The game is played on this = LEDIF   _ _ _ _ _

13. He leads the team = TRAQUEBRACK   _ _ _ _ _ _ _ _ _ _

What is the hardest thing about learning to skate?

This skater has invented a new sport—spelling out words with the blades of her skates! Connect the dots to learn the answer to this important question:

HINT: Try to connect the dots with swooping, curved lines—as if you were skating!

Go Team!

These fans want to show that they are crazy for a certain sport! Follow the directions below to see their message.

1. Fill in all the blocks on the left side of signs 1, 2, 3, 6, 7, 9, 11, 12, 15, 21

2. Fill in all the top squares on signs 2, 3, 5, 6, 9, 11, 15, 16, 21

3. Fill in all the bottom squares of signs 1, 2, 3, 9, 11, 12, 16

4. Fill in all the right squares of signs 1, 6, 11, 12

5. Fill in all the squares down the middle of signs 5 and 8

6. Fill in the very middle square of signs 1, 6, 7, 16, 21

7. Fill in the square just below the middle square of sign 1

8. Copy sign 9 onto sign 18 and 19

9. Copy sign 5 onto sign 13

10. Copy sign 7 onto sign 10

11. Copy sign 2 onto sign 4 and 20

12. Copy sign 11 onto sign 14 and 17

Why do soccer players do well in school?

Use this soccer ball decoder to find out.

Archery Addition

Archibald, Annibelle, and Ace are all shooting at the same target! Can you figure out who is shooting which arrows?

Then, count the points each archer has scored using these rules:

— Add the value of each ring an arrow has stuck into

— Subtract 10 points for any arrow that is on the ground

BONUS: If all of an archer's arrows have stuck in the target, that person gets 5 extra points!

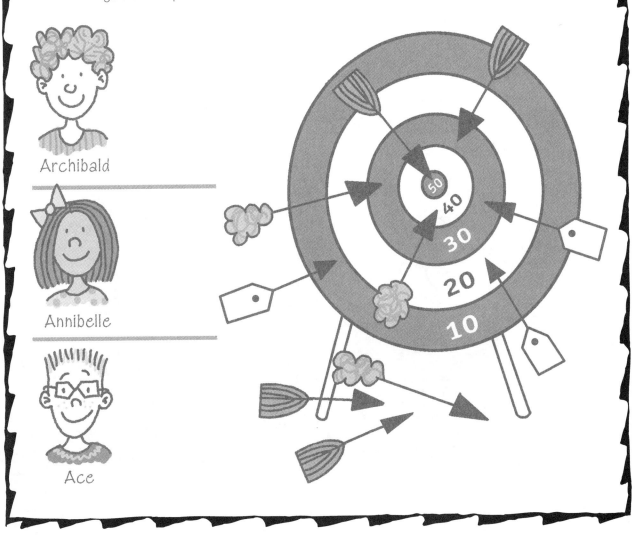

Archibald

Annibelle

Ace

X-treme Sports

Decipher the picture puzzles to find the names of four wild-and-crazy sports!

On Your Mark!

Find the 14 reasons why these kids would be crazy to go swimming!

Goofy Golf

Giorgio loves to play goofy golf. You will, too!
Here are the rules:

- You must go to every hole.
- Count the dots you hit along each path.
  Each dot is worth 5 points.
- Add the value of the hole.
- You get a 20-point bonus on any hole with
  an even-numbered score.

Snake

Windmill

Penguin

Flamingo

Crazy Coach

Coach Wazoo has invented some new and crazy sports! Fill in the letter that matches each new sport with its description.

Which two familiar sports did Coach Wazoo combine to create each crazy sport?

___ **Bassocketcerball**

___ **Gymtennasnistics**

___ **Icefootskatballing**

___ **Tracycckling**

___ **Golarcherfy**

A. Throwing a ball while skating on a frozen field.

B. Using a club to hit small, hard, white balls into a target.

C. Tumbling while hitting a small, fuzzy ball with a racquet.

D. Players kick a black and white ball into an overhead net.

E. Running alongside your bike many times around a track.

Shadow Race

Can you find the shadow pattern that exactly matches this picture of Coach Wazoo?

Now this is fun!

72

Chapter 7

Natural Nonsense

To the Top!

There is only one correct way to hike to the top of this crazy mountain. Starting at the bottom, add the value of two neighboring trees. You may only move to the next level where the tree above has a value that matches the sum.

What is a tornado's favorite party game?

To find out, start at the dot at the top of the tornado. Twist your way down to the ground, picking up every third letter as you go.

Not Hot!

What are the two coldest letters in the alphabet? Fill in all the H-O-Ts and say the two remaining letters out loud.

HOTOTHOTOH
OTHOIOTHOT
THOTOTHCTO
HOTHOTHOOH

The Silly Answer Is "Sunlight!"

What's the silly question? To find out, put each of the letters below in its proper place in the grid. The letters all fit in spaces under their own column, but maybe not in the same order!

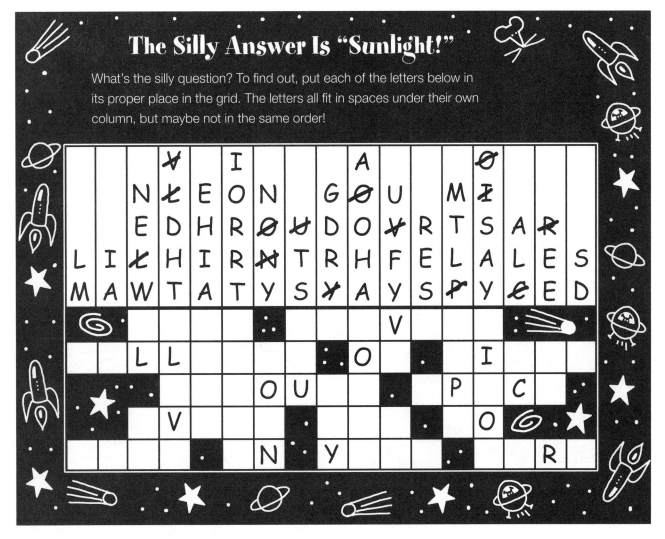

Whoooosh!

Hurricane Harriet scattered Pat's Hat Shop! Can you help put it together again? Start here and find a path that collects the sign, roof, awning, and door. Return them here to the store.

EXTRA: See if you can find the 35 hats that Pat lost!

Wacky Weather

March has all kinds of weather going on! Use these clues to make a picture history. Draw the correct weather symbol on each day.

1. It rained every day that could be evenly divided by 6.

2. A cloudy day always came before a rainy day.

3. There was a snowstorm for two days in the middle of the month, starting on a Saturday.

4. There was only one windy day, exactly in the middle of the month.

5. All the rest of the days were sunny.

CLOUDY

SNOWY

SUNNY

RAINY

WINDY

March

Sun.	Mon.	Tues.	Wed.	Thurs.	Fri.	Sat.
		1	2	3	4	5
6	7	8	9	10	11	12
13	14	15	16	17	18	19
20	21	22	23	24	25	26
27	28	29	30	31	Notes:	

What Is a Tree's Favorite Drink?

Fill in all shapes marked with the letters G-U-L-P to find out!

Hide-and-Seek

Put the animal names scattered on this page into the proper blanks to form new words. **HINT:** Some names can be used more than once, and one won't be used at all!

BEAR

FLY

PIG

BIRD

COW

ANT

DOG

CAT

LION

1. _ _ _ WOOD
2. S _ _ _ _ L
3. MIL _ _ _ _ _
4. _ _ _ EON
5. S _ _ _ TER
6. _ _ _ _ HOUSE
7. _ _ _ BOY
8. STIF _ _ _
9. S _ _ _ OT
10. _ _ _ _ DS

Animal Addition

How do you make a baby frog? Add the answers to each definition and you will create a baby frog—and five other animals, too!

word for soil _____

+ word for pig _____

= a woodchuck _____

breathe quickly _____

+ opposite of him _____

= dark leopard _____

pet you ride _____

+ foot covering _____

+ cranky person _____

= seashore animal _____

role in a play _____

+ chain of hills _____

= game bird _____

pull slowly _____

+ atop = _____

+ move through the air _____

= long, thin insect _____

a small boy _____

+ long, thin piece of wood _____

= baby frog _____

The Silly Answer Is "You"!

What's the silly question? To find out, see if you can figure out where each puzzle piece goes in the empty grid. Then, write the letters in their proper places.

Where's the Weather?

There are 13 weather words hiding in these sentences. Can you find them all?

How independent Kevin is now!

I certainly hope the river runs under our house.

Kami stole the cobra in Concord.

The twins were both under the bed.

Two gruff ogres hum identical tunes.

The Earth ails when recycling fails.

Winston scolds Eric loudly.

The aisle Ethan walked down was skinny.

WORD LIST

fog	humid
cold	hail
ice	cloud
sun	sleet
mist	thunder
rain	wind
snow	

Rain Man, Sun Man

No one wants poor Rain Man at the beach! Can you help him move through the maze until he turns into a sunny day? Make a path that alternates between rain and sun. You can move up and down, or side-to-side, but not diagonally. If you hit a cloudy day, you are going the wrong way!

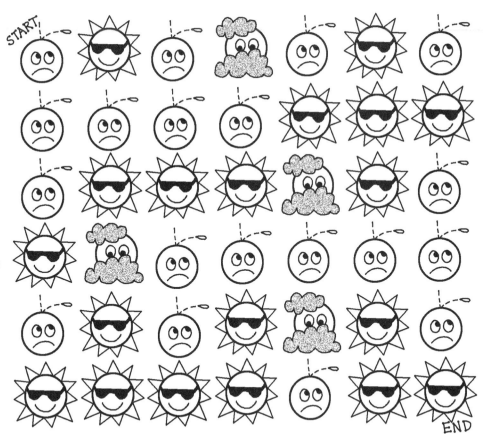

What nickname do weather forecasters call their baby boys?

Use a simple number substitution code (A=1, B=2, C=3 . . .) to find out!

Secret Garden

Gwendolyn's garden is missing a secret ingredient. To complete each word in the grid, add letters from the word E-A-R-T-H. We've given you some hints, but they are not in the same order as the answers! Can you write the number of each hint by its answer?

1. gets cut in summer
2. smells nice
3. falls in Fall
4. freezes in Winter
5. makes walls
6. grows from seeds
7. blooms in Spring
8. grows in pods
9. running water
10. sips flowers
11. eats dirt

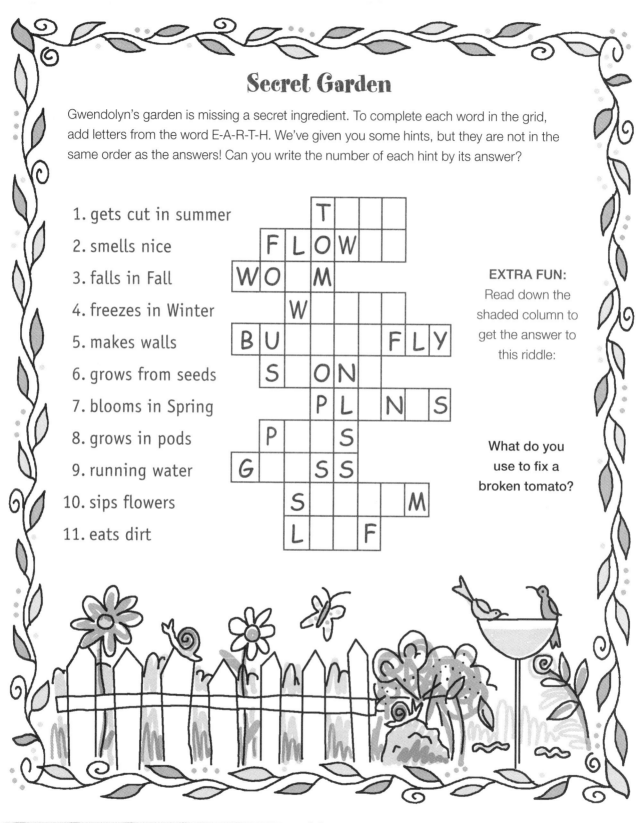

EXTRA FUN:
Read down the shaded column to get the answer to this riddle:

What do you use to fix a broken tomato?

The Silly Answer Is "Water"!

What's the silly question? To find out, use the directions to cross words out of the grid. Read the remaining words from left to right and top to bottom!

Cross out all words that . . .

. . . start with the letter O

. . . rhyme with the word "fair"

. . . are bodies of water

. . . have U in the middle and N at the end

. . . have three letters and no T

CARE	WAS	WIN
ONCE	RUN	WHAT
OCEAN	RUNS	SUN
MAN	WEAR	BEAR
AIR	ONLY	STARE
POND	BUT	FUN
NEVER	BUN	LAKE
CAR	OKAY	WALKS

Zany Rainy

Ramona and Celeste are twins who do everything together, even jumping in puddles! Can you find the 10 differences between the pictures of the girls enjoying a rainy day?

Dark Shadows

The sun was low on the horizon late this afternoon. Can you tell what it is causing to cast these six long, strange shadows? We've given you a few hints, but be careful. There are more hints than shadows!

car boat bike wheelchair giraffe rabbit dog
boy on a ladder cat in a wagon bird on a branch
rocking chair Mervin watering can bottle TV

Chapter 8

Tricky Travels

What Do You Call It . . .

What do you call it when tourists go out dancing in the hot, tropical sun?

Think of words that mean the same thing as each of the words below.
Fill them in the blanks; then read the shaded letters from top to bottom.
HINT: All the words you need rhyme with "quake."

meat = _ _ _ _ _

pain = _ _ _ _

cook = _ _ _ _

snow = _ _ _ _ _

tool = _ _ _ _

phony = _ _ _ _

reptile = _ _ _ _ _ _

male duck = _ _ _ _ _

damage = _ _ _ _ _

dessert = _ _ _ _

error = _ _ _ _ _ _ _

alert = _ _ _ _ _

86

Go! Go! Go!

See how quickly you can travel through this list to fit all the letter sets into their correct spaces!

Not silver = <u>G</u> <u>O</u> _ _

Long dress = <u>G</u> <u>O</u> _ _

Turkey noise = <u>G</u> <u>O</u> _ _ _ _

Large ape = <u>G</u> <u>O</u> _ _ _ _ _

Not hello = <u>G</u> <u>O</u> _ _ _ _ _

A cart = _ _ <u>G</u> <u>O</u> _

Fairytale lizard = _ _ _ <u>G</u> <u>O</u> _

Didn't remember = _ _ _ <u>G</u> <u>O</u> _

Western state = _ _ _ <u>G</u> <u>O</u> _

Spanish friend = _ _ _ <u>G</u> <u>O</u>

Deep blue = _ _ _ _ <u>G</u> <u>O</u>

City in Illinois = _ _ _ _ _ <u>G</u> <u>O</u>

BYE	LD	IN
N	WN	N
DI	AMI	CA
N	LE	BB
FOR	RIL	DRA
T	LA	CHI
ORE	OD	WA

EXTRA FUN:

All these travelers are go, go, going somewhere! Can you find the two cars that are exactly alike? It doesn't matter that the cars are going in different directions.

Peculiar Passport

This passport is strange—all of the country names are written in rebus form! Figure them out and write the real name underneath each country's stamp.

EXTRA STRANGE:

It would be impossible to get your passport stamped in one of these countries today. Do you know which one, and why?

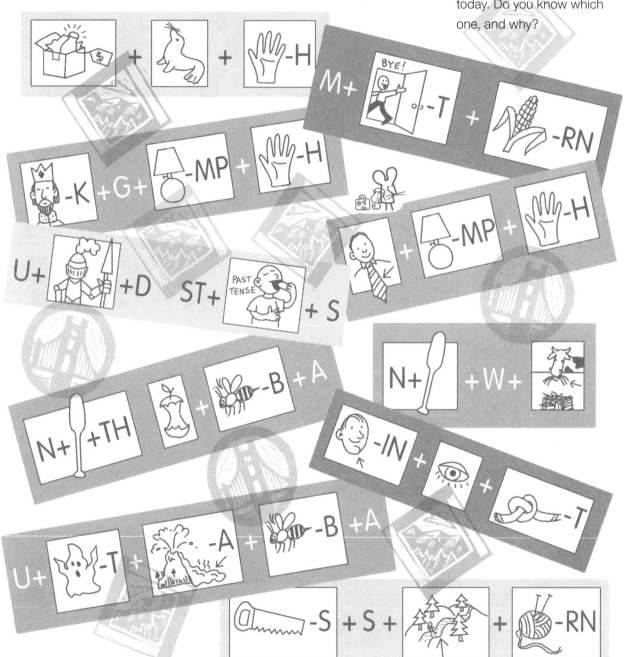

USA, ABC

Three consecutive letters are needed to finish each name of these famous national monuments and parks.

National Monuments

FO_T _UM_ER

_OU_T RUSHM_RE

__AT_E OF LIBERTY

_ASA GRAN__

National Parks

G_EAT _MOKEY MOUN_AINS

VALL_Y _OR_E

C_RLS_AD _AVERNS

PET_IFIED FORE__

END

START

Amazing Liberty

Find your way through the Statue of Liberty from START to END.

Potholes

Each of these sets of words is missing one travel word that will make them into compound words.

_____hog	_____go
_____map	_____pet
_____way	_____fare
_____runner	_____pool
_____side	_____sick

Totally Travel

One letter is needed to finish each of these silly travel sentences. Can you say each one three times fast?

_ eter's _ lane _ owered _ ast _aper _ yramids.

_ om _ ook _ en _ iny _ rains _ o _ oronto.

_ arla's _amera _ aught _amping _amels.

_ teven _ ilently _ ailed _ ideways.

_ ob's _ us _ ounced _ riskly _ ackwards.

_ itch _ errily _aneuvered _ama's _ otorcycle.

Hi-Ho Hink Pinks

Hink Pinks are two single-syllable words that rhyme. Can you come up with the hink pinks that fit these transportation explanations?

Undecorated track-rider = _ _ _ _ _   _ _ _ _ _

Celebrity vehicle = _ _ _ _   _ _ _

Commotion on public transport = _ _ _   _ _ _ _

Not-crazy flying vehicle = _ _ _ _   _ _ _ _ _

Long trip on two-wheeler = _ _ _ _   _ _ _ _

Jacket for floating vehicle = _ _ _   _ _ _ _

Big vehicle for chickens = _ _ _ _ _   _ _ _ _ _

Huge car for hire = _ _ _ _   _ _ _ _

An intelligent, small wagon = _ _ _ _ _   _ _ _ _

What 10-letter word starts with G-A-S?

Use the clues below to learn the answer to this curious question.

The fifth letter ☐

Right after K ☐

Between H and J ☐

Right before C ☐

Right before P ☐

Right after L ☐

Between N and P ☐

Right after S ☐

One before V ☐

The first letter ☐

Oops—did we mention that you must read the answer from bottom to top?

◁ GAS

Why is traveling by boat the cheapest way to get around?

Solve the clues and put the letters in their proper place in the grid until you have the answer to this riddle.

1D	2E	3C	4D	5A	6A	7F
■	8B	9B	10D	11C	12F	■
13B	14C	15A	■	16E	17B	
■	18B	19F	20F	21C	22E	■

A. Shines in the sky

_ _ _
6 5 15

B. Color of mud

_ _ _ _ _
8 13 9 18 17

C. Pretty, charming

_ _ _ _
3 14 11 21

D. Sheep sound

_ _ _
1 4 10

E. Rock, mineral

_ _ _
16 22 2

F. You sit on this

_ _ _ _
12 7 19 20

Out the Window

Malena is looking out the window of the train. She watches the following events roll past. Can you put the pictures in the right sequence so that they make sense?

What has eight wheels and flies?

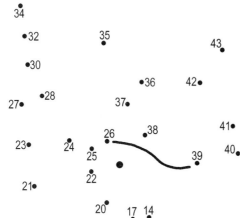 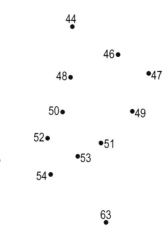 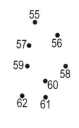

Flying in a plane is a great way to get around, but there are some other pretty crazy ways to take to the skies. Connect the dots in order to see one!

This tropical tourist spot holds a lot more than monkeys and toucans. Look for a bow tie, mitten, ski hat, crown, teacup, kite, eyeglasses, banana, sock, scissors, bunny, spoon, heart, fork, and umbrella!

Hidden Jungle

Time to Get Up!

The Avion family have to get up early to catch a plane. They don't want to oversleep, so everyone sets an alarm clock! Unfortunately, only one clock is set to go off at the correct time. Find the pattern in all the clock times, below. The correct time is halfway between the earliest time and the latest time.

What is the correct time for the Avion family to get up?

Time to Leave!

Catching a plane on time takes a lot of math! Use this information to figure out when you would have to leave for the airport if your plane is at 9:15 A.M.

- 45 minutes to drive to the airport.
- 20 minutes to park and check bags.
- 10 minutes to walk to the gate.
- You need to be at the gate 1 hour before the plane leaves.
- Add an extra 30 minutes, just in case!

94

The Great Race

The Kripp family and the Krumm family are driving cross-country. Both families are starting in Maine, but they are following different routes.

The family with the lowest score wins!

Who will reach the West Coast first? To find out, follow these directions.

- Pick a different color for each family.
- Color the states through which each family will drive.
- Add up the number value for all states with one family's color, then the other.
- Sometimes one state will have two colors. That's OK.

KRIPP FAMILY	OH	ME	NH	VT
	IL	NY	PA	SD
	MT	IN	WI	MN
	OR	ND	ID	

KRUMM FAMILY	TX	PA	ME	MS
	CA	MA	NY	SC
	GA	AZ	NC	NH
	VA	AL	LA	NM

See You Later

No matter where you travel, sooner or later it is time to say goodbye. Can you find each of the following farewells in this around-the-world word search?

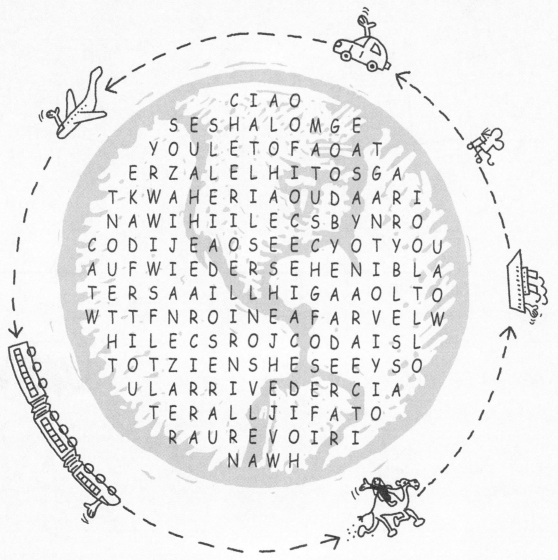

```
          C I A O
        S E S H A L O M G E
      Y O U L E T O F A O A T
    E R Z A L E L H I T O S G A
    T K W A H E R I A O U D A A R I
    N A W I H I I L E C S B Y N R O
  C O D I J E A O S E E C Y O T Y O U
  A U F W I E D E R S E H E N I B L A
  T E R S A A I L L H I G A A O L T O
  W T T F N R O I N E A F A R V E L W
    H I L E C S R O J C O D A I S L
    T O T Z I E N S H E S E E Y S O
    U L A R R I V E D E R C I A
      T E R A L L J I F A T O
        R A U R E V O I R I
          N A W H
```

Adiós (Spanish)

Ciao (Italian)

Arrivederci (Italian)

Zai Jian (Chinese)

Aloha (Hawaiian)

Farvel (Danish)

Hej hej (Danish)

Tofa (Samoan)

Antio (Greek)

Tot ziens (Dutch)

Bless (Icelandic)

Au revoir (French)

Sayonara (Japanese)

Auf Wiedersehen (German)

Tusch (German)

Shalom (Hebrew)

Cheerio (British)

Kwaheri (Swahili)

Goodbye (English)

Chapter 9

Nutty Notations

DREAM

SOME

MADE   RIGHT

OFF   OUT

HOME

ENGLISH

Portrait of A Mouse

MATH 1,2,3

Wanda Wonders

Wanda should be studying, but she has let her mind wander. See if you can follow Wanda's thoughts by figuring out the best word to put in each blank. Follow these directions:

• Start at Wanda and work your way up the word string. Yes, you'll be writing upside-down part of the time!

• The word you add must work with the word on either side of it to form a common phrase or compound.

HINT: Not all of the words are used, and one of them is used twice!

WORD LIST

RUN	TIME
UP	DAY
PUT	FLY
HAND	WORK

Wish Upon a Star

Use a white gel pen or white pencil to connect the dots in order to see what Cassandra is wishing for.

Gnop Gnip

What makes this silly noise? See if you can figure out how to read the amazing answer to this ridiculous riddle!

Gobbledygook

This looks like crazy talk, but these sentences actually make sense! Read each one aloud until you can figure out what it really says.

1. Vat ary ewe due ing?

2. We aris da pahrtty?

3. Eye kan tsea yu enew ear!

4. Vatis yoa rphav o aret kollar?

5. Hoo isy oarb ist fre nde?

Eye ill bet chew can treed iss!

pocketbook into
medical person
to
_____

baked dessert
into garden tool
to

what you read into
curved metal hanger
to

middle of your face
into a flower
to

finger jewelry into
male royalty
to

bird's home into
a sleeveless sweater
to

penny into
portable shelter
to

baby bear into
bathtime place
to

long, soft seat into
a drawstring bag
to

feline pet into
baseball stick
to

dotted cubes into
small rodents
to

street into
cousin of a frog
ROAD to TOAD

teddy into fruit
to

Imagine That!

You can change one thing into another
just by using your imagination! Imagine a
different first letter of each word to get a
completely different thing.

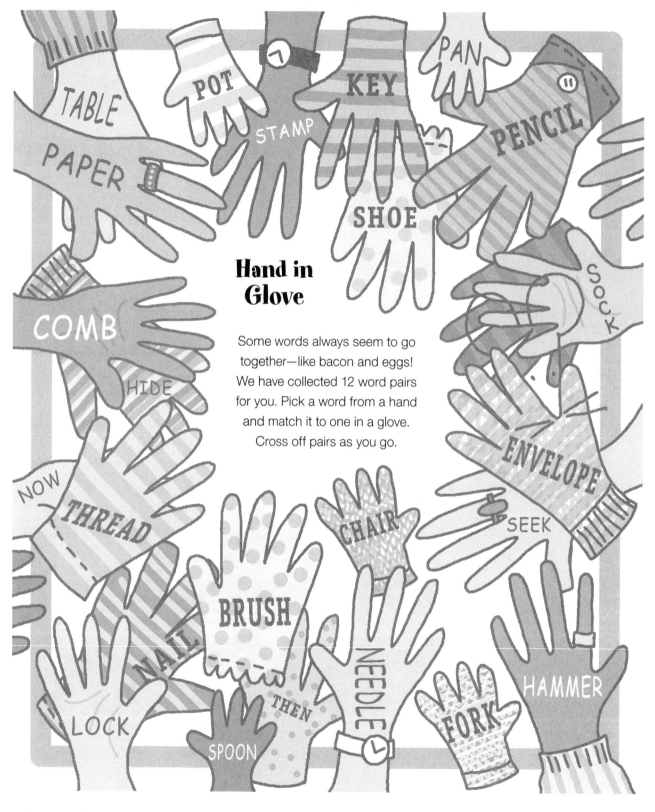

Hand in Glove

Some words always seem to go together—like bacon and eggs! We have collected 12 word pairs for you. Pick a word from a hand and match it to one in a glove. Cross off pairs as you go.

Noble Knight

Hubert likes to imagine he is a knight in shining armor. Five "knightly qualities" are hiding in the letter grid. To find them, pick one letter from each column moving from left to right. Each letter can be used only once. The first has been done for you!

H̶	A	U	O̶	R̶
T	E	N̶	R	K
H	Ø	L	T	T
V	P	A	N	H
S	R	U	O	R

1. HONOR
2. _____
3. _____
4. _____
5. _____

Creative Cook

Francesca can cook everything from soup to nuts! Can you help her? Work from top to bottom. Use the clues to help you decide which one letter in the word to change on each step.

SOUP

— makes bubbles
— to fly up high
— used to row boats
— cereal grains
— big rodents
— grooves in the ground

NUTS

Hopping Harry

Harry hops everywhere he goes, but he will only hop on odd numbers. Help Harry hop down to his friend, Horatio. Harry can hop up, down, left, right, but not diagonally.

							START
8	22	40	25	9	43	66	19
90	39	7	53	32	81	14	51
46	3	18	64	6	77	95	3
12	49	27	17	35	58	12	34
2	10	82	70	19	4	86	27
7	23	41	96	1	18	54	9
11	16	9	44	65	33	17	45
5	38	55	13	3	76	8	20
7	22	12	8	6	13	10	3

END

Curious Question:

Can you hop higher than an elephant?

104

Lotsa Lists

Lyle loves to make lists, but he always abbreviates them!
Using the clues to help, can you write out his complete lists?

Holidays: NY. V. E. 4J. H. T. H. C.

Weather: S. C. R. F. W. S.

Pets: C. D. B. F. G. H. S.

Colors: R. Y. B. G. O. P. B. W.

Vehicles: C. B. T. B. P. M. B.

Quick Catalog

To "catalog" a collection is to make a detailed list of everything that's in it. How quickly can you catalog the 11 three-letter words hiding in the word C-A-T-A-L-O-G?

CATALOG

Triple Triangles

Use the bottom word of each triangle as your letter list. Starting at the top, add one letter at a time to create new words as you move down the triangle.

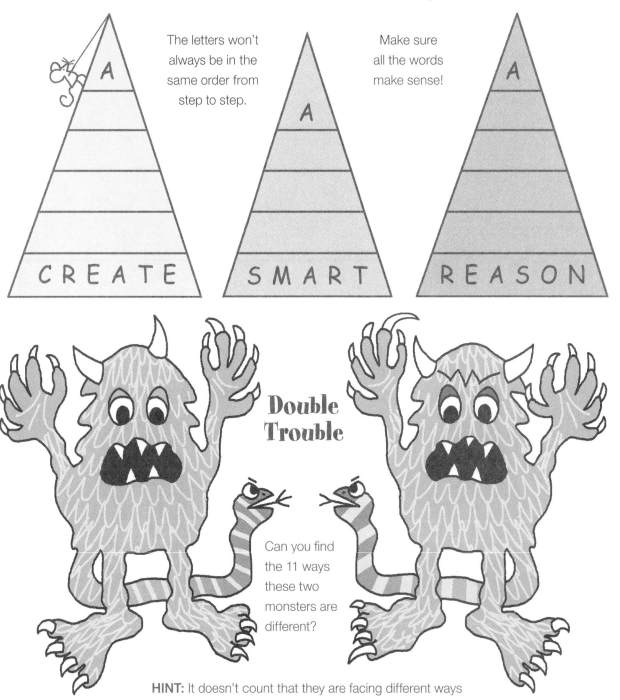

The letters won't always be in the same order from step to step.

Make sure all the words make sense!

A

CREATE

A

SMART

A

REASON

Double Trouble

Can you find the 11 ways these two monsters are different?

HINT: It doesn't count that they are facing different ways

Crossed Creatures

Use the hints below to come up with the names of 14 magical or monstrous creatures. Then see if you can fit them into their proper places in the criss-cross. We left you some M-A-G-I-C and a little M-O-N-S-T-E-R to help out.

Tinkerbell was one

Small, magical helper

Hides under bridges

Sings in the sea

Howls at the moon

Half eagle, half lion

Half man, half horse

Half man, half goat

Tolkien's tree creature

Sleeps all day

Fire breather

Big and tall

One white horn

Lives in gardens

Black or White?

Can you find the figure that is the EXACT opposite of each figure in the box below?
Draw a line to match the pairs.

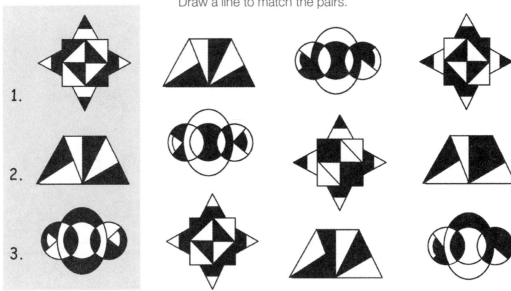

1.

2.

3.

Who's Crazy Now?

These two men have worked together for so long that they have started to speak their own special language. Can you break the code and figure out what they are laughing about?

**WHEEHHEEAHOTHO
DHAOHA   YHEEOHEEUHO
CHOAHALHALHEE   AHEE
CHORHOAHAZHAYHEE
BHEEAHOKHOEHARHA?**

**AHEE DHEEOHOUHOGHAHHA
NHEEUHEETHO!**

Just when you thought the fun was all done, there's more! See if you can find each of these picture pieces somewhere in this book. Write the name of the puzzle each piece is from in the space under each box. **HINT:** There is only one picture piece from each chapter.

1.

2.

3.

4.

5.

6.

7.

8.

9.

Appendix 2: **Online Fun**

There are many family-oriented Web sites that can provide entertainment for kids (of all ages) who like puzzles. Below are listed some of our favorite places on the Internet to visit for online games and puzzles:

www.brainbashers.com
Claims to be the world's most popular puzzle Web site. Has a "puzzle of the day" and adds five new puzzles a week. A huge collection of brain teasers, puzzles, games, and optical illusions.

www.coolopticalillusions.com
This site is loaded with more than 140 different optic tricks and illusions. Some explain how the illusion works, and many can be printed so you can show your friends.

www.funbrain.com
Claims to be the #1 Education Site for K–8 kids and teachers. Search for games by topic—such as art, geography, history, language, technology—or by grade level.

www.jigzone.com
The perfect online site for jigsaw puzzle lovers. Simple to use—just pick a picture and the number of pieces you prefer. Then click the mouse and drag the pieces to their proper place. You can even upload your own photos and turn them into puzzles!

www.kidsdomain.com
A critically acclaimed entertainment and educational site for kids, their parents, and their teachers. Topics covered are space, music, animals, science, and a whole lot more! A great family resource.

www.kidwizard.com
An award-winning, fun, and educational site for kids 6–12 years old. It has a magical slant that focuses on dragons, unicorns, knights, fairies, and the like. Includes mazes, quizzes, logic puzzles, crosswords, word searches, dot-to-dots, and various other types of puzzles.

www.nationalgeographic.com/ngkids/games
All kinds of wild and wacky games, brain teasers, quizzes, and picture puzzles. Includes a game archive full of challenging activities.

www.puzzlechoice.com
This family-friendly site has a "kid's choice" section. It includes crosswords, word searches, picture puzzles, logic puzzles, and more.

page vi • **Funny Faces**

YOUR NAME!

page 2 • **Houses in Houses**

I live in a frame. __PICTURE__
I live in a piggybank. __MONEY__
I live in a vase. __FLOWER__
I live in a carton. __MILK__
I live in a tube. __TOOTHPASTE__
I live in a deck. __CARD__
I live in a trashcan. __GARBAGE__
I live in a book. __BOOKMARK__
I live in a tank. __FISH__

I live in a jar. __COOKIE__
I live in a lamp. __LIGHTBULB__
I live in a box. __TISSUE__
I live in a hamper. __LAUNDRY__
I live in a clock. __CUCKOO__

page 3 • **Knock, Knock!**

1. Anita minute to think it over.
2. Canoe come out and play?
3. Harry up, it's cold out here!
4. Ketchup with me and I'll tell you.
5. Don't you know your own name?

page 4 • **No Way!**

BECAUSE HE CAN'T BE A BROTHER AND A SISTER, TOO.

page 5 • **Silly Sand**

page 5 • **Muddy Madness**

slithery snake tracks
turtle tracks (tail drags between feet)
web-footed goose tracks
BIG elephant tracks

You can tell that the top track is made by the snake because it is shaped like a snake slithering along. The elephant leaves big, round tracks with his big, round feet. The duck leaves triangular-shaped footprints with his webbed feet. The turtle leaves footprints with a wiggly line running down the middle. That's his tail dragging along behind him! You might have thought these were mouse tracks, but look how big they are compared to the other tracks on the floor. A mouse would leave a MUCH smaller bunch of footprints!

PUZZLE ANSWERS

page 6 • Name Game

Art
Alexis
Matt
Angelina
Mark
Abigail
Isaac
Carol
Noah
José

page 7 • Dog in the House

H O U S E
B O A T
T R A I L E R
A P A R T M E N T
H O T E L
C A B I N
D U P L E X

The "dog in the house" is a

M I N I A T U R E
P O O D L E

page 7 • Shy Pets

Can't you catch me?
We allow lots of oxygen here.
The sad ogre ate chili on toast.
I wish arks were floating in my pond.
"Woof" is how Max says hello.
Please grab bits of drab earth.
Caspar rotated the extra tires on his car.

page 8 • That's Different

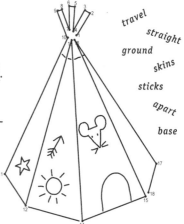

I come apart so I can travel.
I'm covered with skins that
won't unravel. I'm built on
sticks stuck in the ground —
the sticks are straight, but
my base is round!

travel
straight
ground
skins
sticks
apart
base

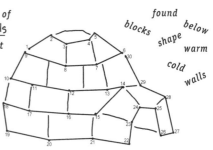

I'm icy cold and made of
snow. Outside my walls
it's 10 below! I'm built
from blocks, but my
shape is round.
Where it's warm,
I won't be found!

found
blocks
below
shape
warm
cold
walls

page 9 • Tidy Cat

A. The ninth letter
I
7

B. Holds up pants
B E L T
12 5 6 3

C. The way out
E X I T
10 14 1 9

D. Opposite of south
N O R T H
2 13 11 8 4

1C	2D		3B	4D	5B
I	N		T	H	E
6B	7A	8D	9C	10C	11D
L	I	T	T	E	R
12B	13D	14C			
B	O	X	!		

112

PUZZLE ANSWERS

page 10 • Who Lives Where?

1. LIGHT HOUSE
2. BIRD HOUSE
3. CARD HOUSE
4. HAUNTED HOUSE
5. GINGERBREAD HOUSE

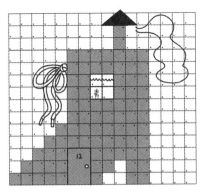

page 11 • What's Weird?

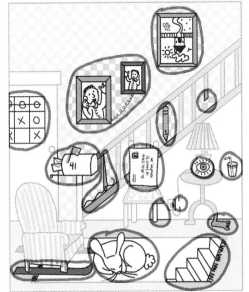

page 12 • The Ha-Ha House

1F, 2E, 3C, 4D, 5A, 6B

page 14 • Autograph Fun

page 15 • Loony Language

Hello, Nadia. What are you up to?

Hello, Aidan. I just got out of school.

Did you have a good day?

No! I had a lot of tests.

That's too bad. Tomorrow will be different.

I hope so!

Well, I have to go. Goodbye!

Goodbye!

page 15 • Friendly Hink Pinks

A girl friend
<u>G</u> <u>A</u> <u>L</u>
<u>P</u> <u>A</u> <u>L</u>

A dirty friend
<u>M</u> <u>U</u> <u>D</u> <u>D</u> <u>Y</u>
<u>B</u> <u>U</u> <u>D</u> <u>D</u> <u>Y</u>

A wonderful friend
<u>G</u> <u>R</u> <u>E</u> <u>A</u> <u>T</u>
<u>M</u> <u>A</u> <u>T</u> <u>E</u>

A sad friend
<u>G</u> <u>L</u> <u>U</u> <u>M</u>
<u>C</u> <u>H</u> <u>U</u> <u>M</u>

page 16 • Almost Twins

color of daisy
curly stem
brim of hat
neck of T-shirt
pocket on overalls
edge of sleeves
belt
length of shorts
stripes on socks
shoes

page 16 • Looks the Same, But...

bass (kind of fish/deep voice); bow (weapon for shooting arrows/to bend forward); lead (heavy, soft metal/to show the way); sewer (one who sews/pipe to carry away waste); wind (air moving across Earth/wrap something around something else); tear (water from the eye/a rip in fabric)

page 17 • Bead Buddies

YOU
ARE
THE
BEST

page 17 • Just Friends

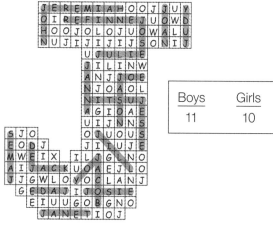

Boys	Girls
11	10

page 18 • Pucker Up

Josie and Arlo will make the same amount of money ($3.50) if they sell all their lemonade!

page 18 • Crazy Keyboard

To decipher each letter, number, or symbol in the message, look down one row, and to the right one key.

Y 9 2   E 9   6 9 7   J 9 F 3
HOW   DO   YOU   MOVE

Q   D 9 2 !   7 W 3   Q
A   COW?   USE   A

J 9 9 F 8 H T   F Q H P
MOOVING   VAN!

PUZZLE ANSWERS

page 19 • Tough for Two

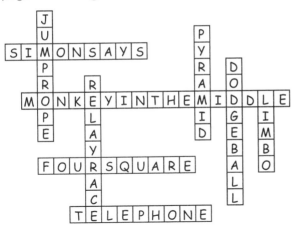

page 20 • Silly Sleepover

The bathtub is a very silly place for a sleepover!

page 21 • Pass It On

What should you do if a teacher rolls his eyes at you? Pick them up and roll them back!

page 22 • Ready, Set, Go!

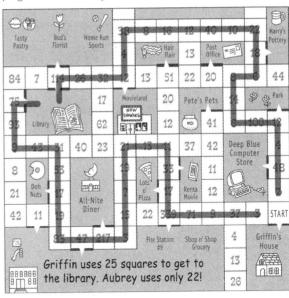

Griffin uses 25 squares to get to the library. Aubrey uses only 22!

page 23 • In the Shadows

page 24 • Friends to the End

F R I E N D = a person you like who likes you

L E N D = to let a person borrow something

B L E N D = to mix together completely

S P E N D = to pay money

L A V E N D E R = pale purple

M E N D = to fix or repair

T E N D E R = kind or loving

A G E N D A = a list of things to be done

D E F E N D = to protect against danger

E X T E N D = to make longer

L E G E N D = story told for many years

O F F E N D = to cause to be angry

E N D L E S S = never stopping

S L E N D E R = long and thin

A P P E N D I X = info at the end of a book

C A L E N D A R = place to write special dates

S P L E N D I D = really awesome

F E N D E R = metal piece over a bike's wheel

page 26 • Birthday Bowling

Total of pins left standing (86) minus total of pins knocked down (74) is 12. Nayib is 12 years old.

page 27 • Happy Half

page 27 • Peculiari-tea

MILK SHAKE

SODA
(Code:
A=1, B=2,
C=3, etc.)

JUICE
(Code: Substitute the
letter before each
letter of the message.)

ICED TEA

page 28 • Hink Pinks

A quick present = S W I F T   G I F T

A not real dessert = F A K E   C A K E

A dumb party activity = L A M E   G A M E

page 28 • Kooky Carnival

Almost everything at this carnival is kooky!

page 29 • Cake-o-licious

COFFEECAKE
MARBLECAKE
CARROTCAKE
FRUITCAKE
DEVILSFOODCAKE
CUPCAKE
ANGELFOODCAKE
POUND
WEDDINGCAKE
CHEESECAKE
UPSIDEDOWNCAKE

page 30 • Why Do Candles . . .

B	E	C	A	U	S	E		Y	O	U
C	A	N'	T		P	U	T			
T	H	E	M		O	N		T	H	E
B	O	T	T	O	M		O	F		
T	H	E		C	A	K	E	!		

page 30 • What Should You . . .

SPIT OUT THE CANDLES!

page 31 • You're Invited

Please come to my party!
Date: Saturday, April 1
Time: 5–7 p.m.
Place: 3223 Eva Ave.
Acaloola, CA
Breakfast will be served.
Wear your clothes
backward!
Hannah Anna

To read the invitation, hold it up to a mirror—it is printed backward! Hannah wanted to have this kind of party because she has two names that are the same spelled backward or forward. Parts of her address can be read either way, too.

PUZZLE ANSWERS

page 31 • Goofy Guests

IMA TROUT
OLIVE OYL
STAR E. NITE
BEN DOVER
AL B. RIGHTBACK
BILL DING
CANDY KANE

page 32 • Crazy Costume

Chloe decided to go as a mermaid!

page 33 • Silly Song

HAPPY BIRTHDAY TO YOU!
HAPPY BIRTHDAY TO YOU!
YOU LOOK LIKE A MONKEY,
AND SMELL LIKE ONE, TOO!

page 34 • Balls of String

T mtutsicatl cthatirts
H bhlhihnd mhahn's hbhlufhf
E esiemoen esaeyes
Y byinygyo
W cwhawrawdes
E feolleow thee eleeaeder
R rrerd lrigrht rgreren rlrigrht
E eleeaepferog
T thot ptotattot
I iduick diuicki goiosie
E heidee eande eseeke
D dstatdudes

page 34 • Find Your Way

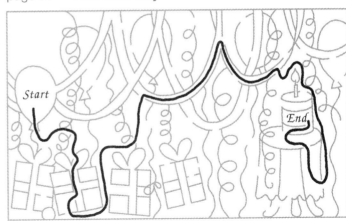

page 35 • Looking for Loot

page 36 • Tons of Fun

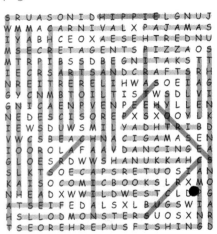

page 38 • Soup's On!

CLAM CHOWDER
Kind of Soup

onions
clams
flour
potatoes
salt
~~dry sand~~
pepper
milk
~~pebbles~~
parsley
butter

CHICKEN
Kind of Soup

water
chicken
pepper
celery
salt
onion
carrots
noodles

VEGETABLE
Kind of Soup

onion
celery
carrots
zucchini
potatoes
tomatoes
green beans
water
salt
pepper
basil

RED, HOW,
WHO, WED,
DEW, HER,
ROW, OWE,
HOE, WOE

page 39 • What a Mouthful

ap´ əl sôs	*applesauce*
kū´ kum bər	*cucumber*
sī´ dər	*cider*
bə nan´ ə	*banana*
kô´ lə flou´ ər	*cauliflower*
brok´ ə lē	*broccoli*
cher´ ē	*cherry*
säl´ sə	*salsa*
sə lä´ mē	*salami*
av´ ə kä´ dō	*avocado*
bā´ ken	*bacon*

page 39 • Berry Good

<u>S T R A W</u> B E R R Y

<u>B L U E</u> B E R R Y

<u>B L A C K</u> B E R R Y

<u>C R A N</u> B E R R Y

<u>R A S P</u> B E R R Y

<u>G O O S E</u> B E R R Y

page 41 • Splash!

page 40 • Where should you go . . .

page 40 • Dizzy Donuts

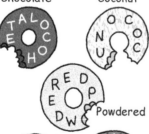

Chocolate   Coconut

Powdered

Glazed   Sprinkled

Dad ate 4 donuts, Mom ate 2, Austin ate 3, Caleb ate 3, and Brooke ate only 1 donut!

page 42 • Crazy Cookies

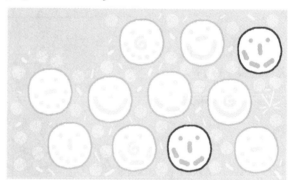

page 42 • What meal do you eat . . .

<u>B</u> A G E L

C E <u>R</u> E A L

Y O G U <u>R</u> T

P A <u>N</u> C A K E

J U I <u>C</u> E

<u>H</u> A M

The answer is:
BRUNCH

page 43 • What's the Difference . . .

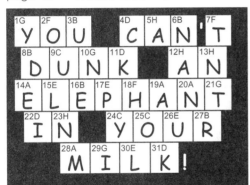

1G	2F	3B		4D	5H	6B	7F
Y	O	U		C	A	N	'T

8B	9C	10G	11D		12H	13H
D	U	N	K		A	N

14A	15E	16B	17E	18F	19A	20A	21G
E	L	E	P	H	A	N	T

22D	23H		24C	25C	26E	27B
I	N		Y	O	U	R

28A	29G	30E	31D
M	I	L	K	!

A. Not nice
M E A N
28 14 19 20

B. Opposite of over
U N D E R
3 6 8 16 27

C. Opposite of me
Y O U
24 25 9

D. Hit with your foot
K I C K
31 22 4 11

E. Opposite of push
P U L L
17 26 30 15

F. Opposite of cold
H O T
18 2 7

G. Really small
T I N Y
21 29 10 1

H. Another name for Grandma
N A N A
13 5 23 12

page 44 • Second Helpings

page 46 • S-L-L-L-L-U-U-U-U-R-R-R-P!

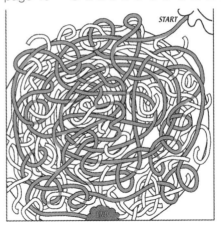

page 47 • How Do You Make . . .

hoT dog   YOgurt   chiPs
Ice cream   hambURger   griLLed cheese
miLk   sAlad
Tuna fish   Taco
   french friEs

Answer: Tilt your plate!

page 47 • Fill 'er Up!

page 48 • Scrambled Eggs

WOOFLES   BACON AND LEGS   SCREAM OF WHEAT

page 48 • Leftovers

CUP **CAKE**
STRAW **BERRY**
POTATO **SALAD**
PEANUT **BUTTER**
POP **CORN**
CORN **CHIPS**
COLE **SLAW**
HOT **DOG**
HAM **BURGER**
FRENCH **FRIES**
TUNA **MELT**
APPLE **SAUCE**
EGG **ROLL**

page 50 • Daffy Descriptions

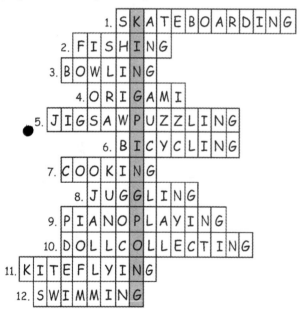

1. SKATEBOARDING
2. FISHING
3. BOWLING
4. ORIGAMI
5. JIGSAWPUZZLING
6. BICYCLING
7. COOKING
8. JUGGLING
9. PIANOPLAYING
10. DOLLCOLLECTING
11. KITEFLYING
12. SWIMMING

page 51 • Take a Hike

WHY IS MOUNTAIN CLIMBING AN EASY HOBBY TO START IF YOU ARE OLD? BECAUSE YOU ARE ALREADY OVER THE HILL!

page 52 • Tacky Ties

page 53 • Too Much Fun

being a clown, riding a unicycle, juggling, reading about cats, photography, listening to music, playing the trumpet, cards, collecting butterflies, collecting stamps

page 53 • Cool Collections

```
S T A M P S H O V E G
F O O S H B I N G P O
F L O C O I N S C A L
X J E L L Y F I S H O
T Y P E S H E L L S H
O K R O W E M O H T A
M A R B L E S M I L E
B A N A T I S S U E S
F O H A T S D U S K Y
S L L O D L P E A S N
O P A L G R E E N Q U
L I G H T B U L B S P
R U N T R R O C K S I
Q S T A P L E S A N D
N O T S E L D O O N O
O V E R D U C A R D S
C O T T O N C A N D Y
S K O O B W O R M S T
```

Might Collect: stamps, coins, shells, rocks, marbles, books, cards, dolls, hats. Would Never Collect: worms, jellyfish, homework, peas, tissues, light bulbs, noodles, staples, cotton candy

page 54 • **Absurd Authors**

7 Learn to Draw
1 Hiking Fun
4 Veggies A to Z
2 Make YOUR OWN Website

5 Your Camera
3 Butterfly Basics
6 MONSTER MADNESS

page 54 • **Camera Chaos**

SHARK   SNAKE   BAT   WALRUS

ARMADILLO   RABBIT   BEAVER   ZEBRA

page 55 • **Movie Night**

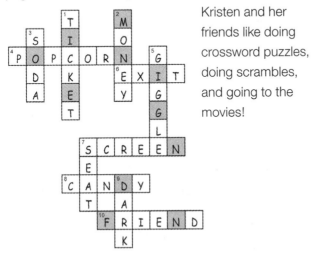

Kristen and her friends like doing crossword puzzles, doing scrambles, and going to the movies!

Kristen and her friends saw *Finding Nemo*.

page 56 • **Whittle Away**

DUCK, Letter A

TURTLE, Letter O

Snowman, Letter P

CAT, Letter S

page 56 • **Totally Tiles**

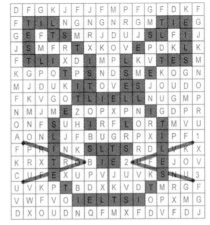

page 57 • **Milo's Magic**

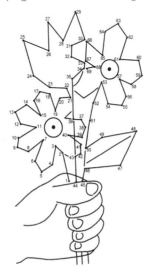

page 57 • Go Fly a Kite

Kaity's kite was red and <u>white</u>. To her <u>delight</u>, it flew to a great <u>height</u>. She hung on <u>tight</u> with all her <u>might</u>, but the kite veered sharply to the <u>right</u>. Snap went the string! "Oh, no!" Kaity cried with <u>fright</u>, as her <u>bright</u> new <u>kite</u> flew out of <u>sight</u>.

page 58 • Loony Tunes

page 59 • Sticky Stamps

1. There are five bird stamps and only four patriotic stamps. 2. Birds are on the most number of stamps. 3. Teddy bears are on the four almost-identical stamps. 4. The stamp with the fox on it has the most postage (.48 cents).

page 60 • What do you ask . . .

T E N T-A C L E S
80 32 56 80 - 8 24 48 32 72

page 60 • Dot's Dominoes

-3 +7 +7 -2 -2 +8 -3 -2 +5 -3 -3
-3   +5
+7   +5
+5   -3
-3 +5 -4 +7 8   START   -4 +6 +6 -1

45. Here's a helpful hint—First make a list of the number of dots on each of the dominoes from START to END. Then go back and add the plus and minus signs according to the rules!

page 62 • Loopy Hoops

Dark Shirts: 212 points
Light Shirts: 201 points

Light shirts win!

page 63 • Happy Camper

1D	2B		3A	4C	5D	6A	7C	
H	E		S	L	E	P	T	
	8A	9B		10B	11C	12A	13B	14C
	A	T		N	I	G	H	T

A. Spaces where something is missing G A P S
12 8 6 3

B. Opposite of now T H E N
9 13 2 10

C. To make crooked T I L T
14 11 4 7

D. Opposite of she H E
1 5

page 63 • What Should You Put . . .

What should you put on
before you get dressed
to be in a relay race?

RUN-DERWEAR!

page 64 • Why does everyone . . .

THEY ARE GREAT
AT CATCHING FLIES!

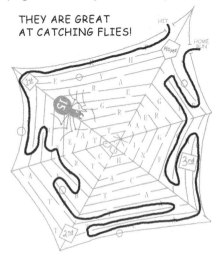

page 65 • Which ghost . . .

1. Player wears this on his head = METHEL — H E L M E T
2. Score! = CHDOTOUWN — T O U C H D O W N
3. To handle clumsily = LEBMUF — F U M B L E
4. To bring a player to the ground = CAKTEL — T A C K L E
5. Shirt with a number on it = SERJYE — J E R S E Y
6. To receive the ball = CHATC — C A T C H
7. Midway through the game = METIHAFL — H A L F T I M E
8. Important January game = PRUES LOWB — S U P E R B O W L
9. Throw ball to another player = SAPS — P A S S
10. Catch ball meant for other team = CEPTERINT — I N T E R C E P T
11. Three feet = DAYR — Y A R D
12. The game is played on this = LEDIF — F I E L D
13. He leads the team = TRAQUEBRACK — Q U A R T E R B A C K

page 66 • What is the hardest . . .

page 67 • Go Team!

page 68 • Why do soccer...

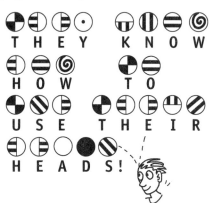

THEY KNOW
HOW TO
USE THEIR
HEADS!

page 69 • Archery Addition

Archibald
```
  30
+ 40
----
  70
- 10
----
  60
```

Annibelle
```
  50
+ 30
----
  80
- 20
----
  60
```

Ace
```
  30
+ 20
+ 10
----
  60
+  5 (bonus)
----
  65
```

page 70 • X-treme Sports

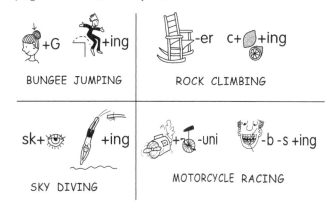

BUNGEE JUMPING

ROCK CLIMBING

SKY DIVING

MOTORCYCLE RACING

page 70 • On Your Mark!

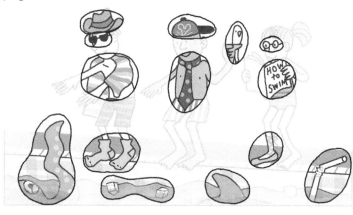

page 71 • Goofy Golf

Snake: 153 pts. (no bonus)

Penguin: 147 pts. (no bonus)

Flamingo: 122 pts. + 20 pt. bonus = 142

Windmill: 114 pts. + 20 pt. bonus = 134

page 72 • Crazy Coach

D **Bassocketcerball**
Basketball and Soccer

C **Gymtennasnistics**
Gymnastics and Tennis

A **Icefootskatballing**
Ice Skating and Football

E **Tracycckling**
Track and Cycling

B **Golarcherfy**
Golf and Archery

page 72 • Shadow Race

page 74 • What is a tornado's favorite party game?

TWISTER!

page 74 • To the Top!

page 75 • Not Hot!

HOTOTHOTOH
OTHOIOTHOT
THOTOTHCTO
HOTHOTHOOH

page 75 • The Silly Answer Is "Sunlight"!

WHAT TRAVELS
MILLIONS OF MILES
THROUGH SPACE
EVERY DAY TO
LAND IN YOUR YARD

page 76 • Whoooosh!

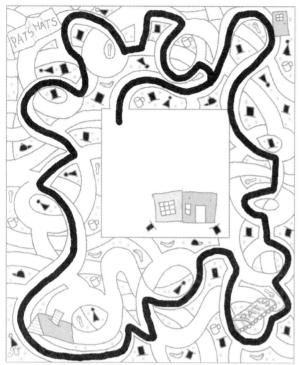

page 77 • Wacky Weather

March

Sun.	Mon.	Tues.	Wed.	Thurs.	Fri.	Sat.
		1 ☀	2 ☀	3 ☀	4 ☀	5 ☁
6 ☂	7 ☀	8 ☀	9 ☀	10 ☀	11 ☁	12 ☂
13 ☀	14 ☀	15 ☀	16 🪁	17 ☁	18 ☂	19 ⛄
20 ⛄	21 ☀	22 ☀	23 ☁	24 ☂	25 ☀	26 ☀
27 ☀	28 ☀	29 ☁	30 ☂	31 ☀	*Notes:* A very nice month!	

page 78 • What Is a Tree's Favorite Drink?

page 78 • Hide-and-Seek

1. <u>D O G</u> WOOD
2. S <u>C</u> OWL
3. MIL <u>L I O N</u>
4. P <u>I</u> G EON
5. S C <u>AT</u> TER
6. <u>B I R D</u> HOUSE
7. C <u>O W</u> BOY
8. STIF <u>F L Y</u>
9. S P <u>I</u> G OT
10. <u>B E A R</u> DS

page 79 • Animal Addition

word for soil	GROUND
+ word for pig	HOG
= a woodchuck	GROUNDHOG

breathe quickly	PANT
+ opposite of him	HER
= dark leopard	PANTHER

pet you ride	HORSE
+ foot covering	SHOE
+ cranky person	CRAB
= seashore animal	HORSESHOE CRAB

role in a play	PART
+ chain of hills	RIDGE
= game bird	PARTRIDGE

pull slowly	DRAG
+ atop =	ON
+ move through the air	FLY
= long, thin insect	DRAGONFLY

a small boy	TAD
+ long, thin piece of wood	POLE
= baby frog	TADPOLE

page 80 • The Silly Answer Is "You"!

W	H	A	T		L	O	O	K	S		L	I	K	E
A		M	O	N	K	E	Y	,		C	A	N		B	E
	F	O	U	N	D		I	N		Z	O	O	S	,
A	N	D		I	S		A	S		L	A	R	G	E
A	S		A		H	U	M	A	N		C	H	I	L	D |?

page 81 • What nickname do . . .

SUNNY!

page 80 • Where's the Weather?

How independent Kevin is now!

I certainly hope the river runs under our house.

Kami stole the cobra in Concord.

The twins were both under the bed.

Two gruff ogres hum identical tunes.

The Earth ails when recycling fails.

Winston scolds Eric loudly.

The aisle Ethan walked down was skinny.

page 82 • Secret Garden

1. gets cut in summer — 7. TREE
2. smells nice — 2. FLOWER
3. falls in Fall — 11. WORM
4. freezes in Winter — 4. WATER
5. makes walls — 10. BUTTERFLY
6. grows from seeds — 5. STONE
7. blooms in Spring — 6. PLANTS
8. grows in pods — 8. PEAS
9. running water — 1. GRASS
10. sips flowers — 9. STREAM
11. eats dirt — 3. LEAF

page 81 • Rain Man, Sun Man

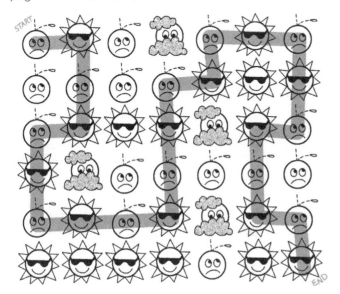

page 83 • The Silly Answer Is "Water"!

CARE	WAS	WIN
ONCE	RUN	(WHAT)
OCEAN	(RUNS)	SUN
MAN	WEAR	BEAR
AIR	ONLY	STARE
POND	(BUT)	FUN
(NEVER)	BUN	LAKE
CAR	OKAY	(WALKS)

page 83 • Zany Rainy

page 84 • Dark Shadows

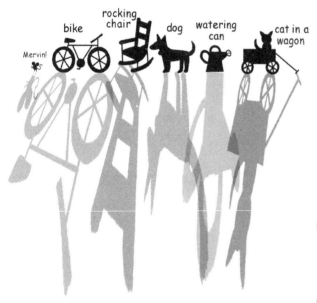

page 86 • What Do You Call It . . .

meat = **S** T E A K

pain = **A** C H E

cook = **B** A K E

snow = **F** L A K E

tool = **R** A K E

phony = **F** A K E

reptile = **S** N A K E

male duck = **D** R A K E

damage = **B** R E A K

dessert = **C** A K E

error = **M** I S T A K E

alert = **A** W A K E

page 87 • Go! Go! Go!

Not silver = G O L D

Long dress = G O W N

Turkey noise = G O B B L E

Large ape = G O R I L L A

Not hello = G O O D B Y E

A cart = W A G O N

Fairytale lizard = D R A G O N

Didn't remember = F O R G O T

Western state = O R E G O N

Spanish friend = A M I G O

Deep blue = I N D I G O

City in Illinois = C H I C A G O

page 88 • Peculiar Passport

New Zealand
England Mexico
United States Thailand
North Korea Norway
Yugoslavia China
Australia

In 2003, the country of Yugoslavia was renamed Serbia and Montenegro. This happened after Yugoslavia's 10-year civil war.

page 89 • USA, ABC

National Monuments

F O R T   S U M <u>T</u> E R
<u>M</u> O <u>U</u> N T   R U S H M <u>O</u> R E
<u>S</u> T A T <u>U</u> E   O F   L I B E R T Y
<u>C</u> A S A   G R A N <u>D E</u>

National Parks

G <u>R</u> E A T   <u>S</u> M O K E Y   M O U N <u>T</u> A I N S
V A L L <u>E</u> Y   <u>F</u> O R <u>G</u> E
C A R L S <u>B</u> A D   <u>C</u> A V E R N S
P E T <u>R</u> I F I E D   F O R E <u>S T</u>

page 89 • Potholes

<u>road</u> hog   <u>car</u> go
<u>road</u> map   <u>car</u> pet
<u>road</u> way   <u>car</u> fare
<u>road</u> runner   <u>car</u> pool
<u>road</u> side   <u>car</u> sick

page 89 • Amazing Liberty

page 90 • Totally Travel

<u>P</u> eter's <u>P</u> lane <u>P</u> owered <u>P</u> ast <u>P</u> aper <u>P</u> yramids.
<u>T</u> om <u>T</u> ook <u>T</u> en <u>T</u> iny <u>T</u> rains <u>T</u> o <u>T</u> oronto.
<u>C</u> arla's <u>C</u> amera <u>C</u> aught <u>C</u> amping <u>C</u> amels.
<u>S</u> teven <u>S</u> ilently <u>S</u> ailed <u>S</u> ideways.
<u>B</u> ob's <u>B</u> us <u>B</u> ounced <u>B</u> riskly <u>B</u> ackwards.
<u>M</u> itch <u>M</u> errily <u>M</u> aneuvered <u>M</u> ama's <u>M</u> otorcycle.

page 90 • Hi-Ho Hink Pinks

Undecorated track-rider = P L A I N   T R A I N

Celebrity vehicle = S T A R   C A R

Commotion on public transport = B U S   F U S S

Not-crazy flying vehicle = S A N E   P L A N E

Long trip on two-wheeler = B I K E   H I K E

Jacket for floating vehicle = B O A T   C O A T

Big vehicle for chickens = C L U C K   T R U C K

Huge car for hire = M A X I   T A X I

An intelligent, small wagon = S M A R T   C A R T

page 91 • What 10-letter word . . .

The fifth letter	E
Right after K	L
Between H and J	I
Right before C	B
Right before P	O
Right after L	M
Between N and P	O
Right after S	T
One before V	U
The first letter	A

page 91 • Why is traveling by boat . . .

1D	2E	3C	4D	5A	6A	7F
B	E	C	A	U	S	E

8B	9B	10D	11C	12F
B	O	A	T	S

13B	14C	15A		16E	17B
R	U	N		O	N

18B	19F	20F	21C	22E
W	A	T	E	R

page 91 • Why is traveling by boat . . . (continued)

A. Shines in the sky

S U N
6 5 15

B. Color of mud

B R O W N
8 13 9 18 17

C. Pretty, charming

C U T E
3 14 11 21

D. Sheep sound

B A A
1 4 10

E. Rock, mineral

O R E
16 22 2

F. You sit on this

S E A T
12 7 19 20

page 92 • Out the Window

page 92 • What has eight wheels and flies?

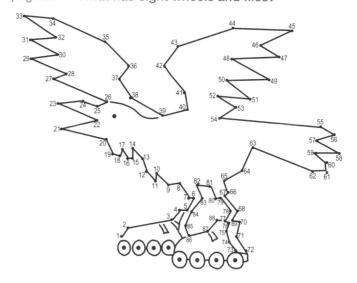

page 93 • Hidden Jungle

page 94 • Time to Get Up!

The correct time for the Avion family to get up is 5:45 A.M.

page 94 • Time to Leave!

The correct time to leave for the airport is 6:30 A.M.

page 95 • The Great Race

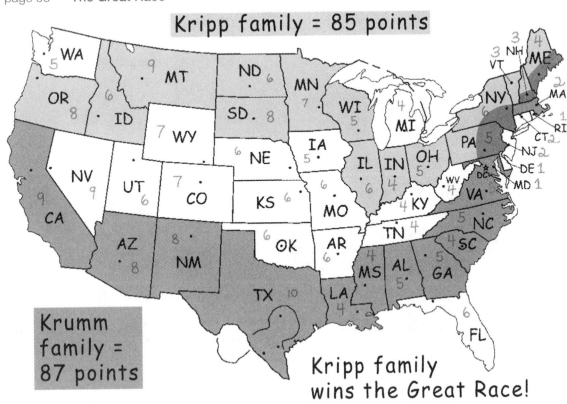

Kripp family = 85 points

Krumm family = 87 points

Kripp family wins the Great Race!

PUZZLE ANSWERS

page 96 • See You Later

page 99 • Wish upon a Star

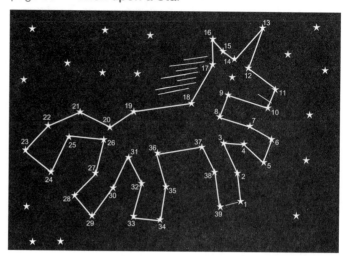

page 98 • Wanda Wonders

page 100 • Gnop Gnip

Hold the book up to a mirror, and tilt the top edge of the book slightly toward you. You will see that the message reads" "A ping pong ball bouncing backward!"

page 100 • Gobbledygook

1. What are you doing?
2. Where is the party?
3. I can't see you anywhere!
4. What is your favorite color?
5. Who is your best friend?

page 101 • Imagine That!

pocketbook into medical person
PURSE to NURSE

baked dessert into garden tool
CAKE to RAKE

what you read into curved metal hanger
BOOK to HOOK

middle of your face into a flower
NOSE to ROSE

finger jewelry into male royalty
RING to KING

bird's home into a sleeveless sweater
NEST to VEST

baby bear into bathtime place
CUB to TUB

long, soft seat into a drawstring bag
COUCH to POUCH

penny into portable shelter
CENT to TENT

feline pet into baseball stick
CAT to BAT

dotted cubes into small rodents
DICE to MICE

street into cousin of a frog
ROAD to TOAD

teddy into fruit
BEAR to PEAR

page 103 • Creative Cook

SOUP	
SOAP	makes bubbles
SOAR	to fly up high
OARS	used to row boats
OATS	cereal grains
RATS	big rodents
RUTS	grooves in the ground
NUTS	

page 102 • Hand in Glove

paper and pencil, comb and brush, stamp and envelope, hammer and nail, table and chair, sock and shoe, pot and pan, key and lock, spoon and fork, needle and thread, hide and seek, now and then

page 103 • Noble Knight

H̶	A	U	O̶	R̶
T	E	N̶	R	K
H	O̶	L	T	T
V	P	A	N	H
S	R	U	O	R

1. HONOR
2. TRUTH
3. HEART
4. VALOR
5. SPUNK

page 104 • Hopping Harry

							START
8	22	40	**25**	**9**	**43**	66	**19**
90	**39**	**7**	**53**	32	**81**	14	**51**
46	**3**	18	64	6	**77**	**95**	**3**
12	**49**	**27**	**17**	**35**	58	12	34
2	10	82	70	**19**	4	86	27
7	**23**	**41**	96	**1**	18	54	9
11	16	**9**	44	**65**	33	17	45
5	38	**55**	**13**	**3**	76	8	20
7 END	22	12	8	6	13	10	3

page 105 • **Lotsa Lists**

1. Holidays: New Year's, Valentine's, Easter, Fourth of July, Halloween, Thanksgiving, Hanukkah, Christmas
2. Weather: Sunny, cloudy, rainy, foggy, windy, snowy
3. Pets: Cat, dog, bird, fish, gerbil or guinea pig, horse or hamster, snake
4. Colors: Red, yellow, blue, green, orange, purple, black, white
5. Vehicles: Car, bus, train, bike, plane, motorcycle, boat

page 105 • **Quick Catalog**

cot, cat, log, tag, got, lot, lag, oat, ago, cog, gal. Did you happen to find a coat and a goat and a goal hiding in the catalog, too?

page 106 • **Triple Triangles**

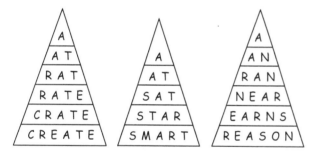

page 106 • **Double Trouble**

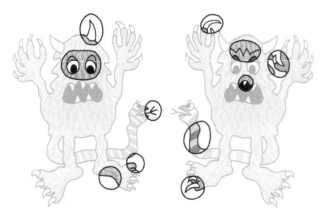

page 107 • **Crossed Creatures**

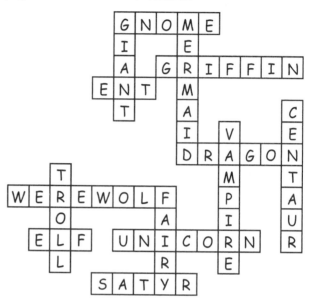

page 108 • **Black or White?**

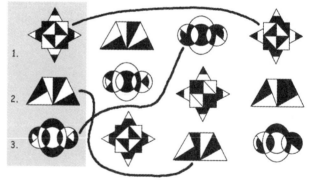

page 108 • Who's Crazy Now?

WHAT
DO YOU
CALL A
CRAZY BAKER?

A DOUGH NUT!

page 109 • **Look Again**

1. Shy Pets

2. Friends to the End

3. Kooky Carnival

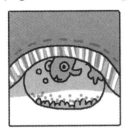

4. Splash!

5. Sticky Stamps

6. Loopy Hoops

7. Secret Garden

8. Hidden Jungle

9. Crossed Creatures

The Everything® KIDS' Series!

Packed with tons of information, activities, and puzzles, the Everything® Kids' books are perennial bestsellers that keep kids active and engaged.

Each book is two-color, 8" x 9¼", and 144 pages.

All this at the incredible price of $6.95!

The Everything® Kids' Crazy
Puzzles Book
1-59337-361-9

The Everything® Kids'
Dinosaurs Book
1-59337-360-0

A silly, goofy, and undeniably icky addition to
the Everything® Kids' series . . .

The Everything® Kids'
GROSS
Series

Chock-full of sickening entertainment for hours of disgusting fun.

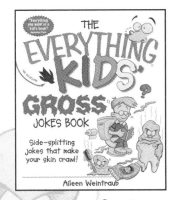

The Everything® Kids' Gross
Jokes Book
1-59337-448-8

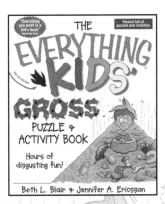

The Everything® Kids' Gross
Puzzle & Activity Book
1-59337-447-X

Other Everything® Kids' Titles Available

The Everything® Kids' Animal Puzzle & Activity Book
1-59337-305-8

The Everything® Kids' Baseball Book, 3rd Ed.
1-59337-070-9

The Everything® Kids' Bible Trivia Book
1-59337-031-8

The Everything® Kids' Bugs Book
1-58062-892-3

The Everything® Kids' Christmas Puzzle &
Activity Book
1-58062-965-2

The Everything® Kids' Cookbook
1-58062-658-0

The Everything® Kids' Halloween Puzzle &
Activity Book
1-58062-959-8

The Everything® Kids' Hidden Pictures Book
1-59337-128-4

The Everything® Kids' Joke Book
1-58062-686-6

The Everything® Kids' Knock Knock Book
1-59337-127-6

The Everything® Kids' Math Puzzles Book
1-58062-773-0

The Everything® Kids' Mazes Book
1-58062-558-4

The Everything® Kids' Money Book
1-58062-685-8

The Everything® Kids' Nature Book
1-58062-684-X

The Everything® Kids' Puzzle Book
1-58062-687-4

The Everything® Kids' Riddles
& Brain Teasers Book
1-59337-036-9

The Everything® Kids' Science Experiments Book
1-58062-557-6

The Everything® Kids' Sharks Book
1-59337-304-X

The Everything® Kids' Soccer Book
1-58062-642-4

The Everything® Kids' Travel Activity Book
1-58062-641-6

Available wherever books are sold!
To order, call 800-258-0929, or visit us at *www.everything.com*
Everything® and everything.com® are registered trademarks of F+W Publications, Inc..